"Rick Stiggins has done an amazing job capturing in plain language and heartwarming stories what so many organizations, think tanks, school districts, and others have been struggling to articulate—that is, the importance of cultivating student self-efficacy through transparency, ongoing feedback, and quality assessment methods. He does a masterful job articulating what many practitioners and school leaders have long been saying—we have to stop treating the process of assessment like a 'gotcha' and create systems that value transparency and fuel student motivation and confidence. With appropriate standards and guidelines, we can create processes *alongside* our students (and even families and communities) to assess and drive student learning."

—Chris DonFrancesco
Senior Policy Analyst
Education Policy and Practice, NEA

"With a career that has consistently challenged our traditional thinking about assessment, Rick Stiggins lays out a compelling vision for assessment with students at the center of the action. The core of the book is assessment *for* learning, where students monitor and manage their own understanding and growth, not just the teacher. This book is an amazing read, especially in the way it speaks directly to students, teachers, school leaders, families, the community, and policy makers. Stiggins also humanizes assessment by digging into emotions, confidence, and relationships . . . and by telling his own learning story! In doing so, he makes us all think about our own journey and how we have been impacted, in both good and bad ways, by curriculum, instruction, and assessment."

—Timothy Dohrer
Director, Teacher Leadership
Northwestern University

"Last year Rick Stiggins conducted a professional develop-ment seminar in my district. I attended that session after which he invited me to provide feedback on a draft of his new book. I was surprised to discover that his manuscript perfectly described the same assessment *for* teaching and learning strategy used by the U.S. Army since 1980 to eval-uate and train each individual and unit. I am a retired Army officer, with thirty years of experience training and leading U.S. Army combat units. As a commander, operations and training officer, and director of a major U.S. Army school, I know that Stiggins's assessment strategy works. His book describes assessment based on research in a manner that is understandable and compelling to the board members so we can allocate resources for training for administrators and faculty with little prior understanding of complex assess-ment practices. In short, this book should be provided to every school board member interested in a coherent strat-egy to improve student academic performance."

—Richard P. Geier, Colonel, U.S. Army (Ret.)
School Board Member
Beaufort County (South Carolina) School District

"For students, confidence comes from understanding what they are required to know and be able to do to master the standards being taught. Formative assessments *for* learning, as Rick Stiggins defines and applies them, can give them that understanding. This puts students in control of their learning. I have been a teacher, school administrator, dis-trict director of transformation schools, assistant superin-tendent, and regional superintendent and now am a current sitting superintendent trying to accelerate student learning after the COVID-19 pandemic and its impact on students. What I find profoundly impactful in Stiggins's book is the power that my faculty and I can derive from building stu-dent confidence by making sure that they understand the end goal of their instruction, where they are now in rela-tion to those expectations, and how they can close the gap between those two keys to their success. If students have a clear understanding of these, it will reduce their anxiety, the key to building confidence. As Stiggins so aptly puts it, 'Successful learning in any context is as much about emotion as it is about cognition,' and 'Good teaching is as much about managing student emotions as it is about managing instructional strategies.'"

—Frank Rodriguez
School District Superintendent
Beaufort County (South Carolina) School District

"This book is a must-have for parents, teachers, intervention teams, school leaders, and educational policy makers seeking to define the path to success for our children and students. Rick Stiggins poignantly weaves real-life experiences and years of research into simple logical tools for teachers, parents, and intervention teams to empower the student to be successful, confident, resilient, and self-reliant and approach learning with joy and enthusiasm. The simple tools for success are clearly outlined, giving parents, teachers, students, and intervention teams an approach to learning by supporting our students through clear goals, transparency, and guidance in the path to reach those goals, as well as ample successes along the way, leading to confidence resulting in students' ability to be responsible, passionate, resilient, and successful lifelong learners. It's a must-read for every educator and parent simplifying how we can align to truly give our children the gift of confidence."

—Kim Harley
Parent
Beaverton, Oregon

"Based on his own personal experience, Rick Stiggins describes how the often overlooked dynamic of the emotional health of the student affected his confidence, ability to learn, and overall self-esteem. This was especially relevant to me since my own grandson broke down in tears when extensive testing revealed he had severe dyslexia and was otherwise highly intelligent. He tearfully admitted that he had always considered himself to be 'stupid.' Knowing that his intelligence was normal and after receiving the tools and support to overcome his dyslexia, his anxiety went away, his sleep improved, his self-esteem skyrocketed, and he became much more comfortable and successful in school. This book is crucial reading for all teachers and administrators, but it is especially important for those involved in serving students with special needs. Stiggins describes how the self-inflicted hopelessness of a struggling learner can affect not only their academic future, but also their perception of their place in society. He speaks for teachers and parents who want educational leaders to supply them with the tools they need to prevent potentially devastating loss of self-esteem and to build in students the desire to pursue the knowledge they will need to succeed in life. This is a critically important book that will motivate and guide parents, teachers, and PTA leaders to join with their students to advocate that local, state, and federal educational policy makers supply teachers with strategies to recognize learning disorders and teaching methods to help every student reach their targets with confidence, self-esteem, and pride."

—Roger Wickland
Grandfather
Portland, Oregon

"It is a rare book that is simultaneously inspirational and practical. *Give Our Students the Gift of Confidence* meets that challenge in a profound and personal way. Rick Stiggins brings us back to the essence of student learning—authentic engagement of students in their own learning. He reminds us that students neither succeed through authoritarian demands, threats, and intimidation nor with false assurances that failure is fine as long as students feel good about themselves. Rather, he encourages educators and parents to challenge the students we serve, confident that students are supremely capable of school success if only we give them the support, encouragement, empowerment, and love that each deserves. Finally, Stiggins balances rigorous research with personal reflections that are deeply moving. If you don't shed a tear for Little Rick, then you won't cry at the end of *Charlotte's Web*. This book will make you think, reflect, and, most importantly, act."

—Douglas Reeves
Author, *Fearless Schools*

Give Our Students the Gift of
Confidence

*Over the past forty years, a new idea has been growing within me.
It has been enriched by my teachers. They helped me come to see
that schooling must be about placing students in charge of their own
learning success. This book is dedicated to those teachers, especially
Doris Sperling, Anne Davies, Jim Popham, Jan Chappuis,
Steve Chappuis, and Ruth Sutton.*

Give Our Students the Gift of

Confidence

It's Essential for Learning Success

Rick Stiggins

A Sage Company

FOR INFORMATION:

Corwin
A SAGE Company
2455 Teller Road
Thousand Oaks, California 91320
(800) 233-9936
www.corwin.com

SAGE Publications Ltd.
1 Oliver's Yard
55 City Road
London, EC1Y 1SP
United Kingdom

SAGE Publications India Pvt. Ltd.
Unit No 323-333, Third Floor, F-Block
International Trade Tower Nehru Place
New Delhi – 110 019
India

SAGE Publications Asia-Pacific Pte. Ltd.
18 Cross Street #10-10/11/12
China Square Central
Singapore 048423

Vice President and Editorial Director:
    Monica Eckman
Publisher: Jessica Allan
Content Development Manager:
    Lucas Schleicher
Content Development Editor:
    Mia Rodriguez
Senior Editorial Assistant: Natalie Delpino
Editorial Intern: Lex Nunez
Production Editor: Tori Mirsadjadi
Copy Editor: Melinda Masson
Typesetter: Exeter Premedia Services
Cover Designer: Gail Buschman
Marketing Manager: Olivia Bartlett

Printed in Canada

Library of Congress Cataloging-in-Publication Data

Names: Stiggins, Richard J., author.
Title: Give our students the gift of confidence : it's essential for learning success / Rick Stiggins.
Description: Thousand Oaks, California : Corwin Press, [2024] | Includes bibliographical references and index.
Identifiers: LCCN 2023024046 (print) | LCCN 2023024047 (ebook) | ISBN 9781071924037 (paperback) | ISBN 9781071924068 (ebook)
Subjects: LCSH: Learning, Psychology of. | Confidence in children. | Educational psychology. | Educational leadership. | Academic achievement. | Teacher-student relationships.
Classification: LCC LB1060 .S8435 2024 (print) | LCC LB1060 (ebook) | DDC 370.117--dc23/eng/20230707
LC record available at https://lccn.loc.gov/2023024046
LC ebook record available at https://lccn.loc.gov/2023024047

This book is printed on acid-free paper.

23 24 25 26 27 10 9 8 7 6 5 4 3 2 1

Contents

Foreword

Rick Stiggins based this wonderful book on three fundamental premises. These premises have a long history of coming in and going out of fashion in education. Each has been, at times, at the forefront of educators' consciousness and, at other times, nearly forgotten. Together they offer profound implications for how we think about teaching and learning, the way we organize schools, and the criteria by which we judge our success as educators.

The first premise stems from the way we define "curriculum." Learning in any subject area or academic discipline is infinite. There is no limit to what knowledge and skills an individual can acquire in any area of study. However, a curriculum is finite. When educators and subject-area experts set forth a curriculum, they specify the subset of content and skills within that infinite body of knowledge that they believe is most important for students to learn. Having delineated that finite curriculum, the job of educators is to ensure that all students learn that curriculum excellently. Not just some. Not just those who are gifted or have special academic talents. Not just those who are privileged or economically advantaged. Not just those who come from stable homes with supportive parents and families. All students! It makes no sense that educators and subject-area experts would develop a curriculum to include things that some students would not be expected to learn well.

Of course, this idea that all students can and should learn excellently is not new in education. Its roots can be traced to the hallmark work of Benjamin Bloom over a half century ago. Rather than focusing on equality of educational opportunities, Bloom argued we should focus on equity in education results. Although students enter school with vastly different backgrounds and experiences that require different approaches to instruction, our task as educators is to ensure that all students learn well, regardless of those initial differences. In developing the instructional process that he labeled "mastery learning," Bloom (1968) showed that with sufficient time and appropriate help, nearly all students could reach a high level of mastery. The primary responsibility of educators, therefore, is to provide the time and appropriate help needed to guarantee that all students do learn excellently the knowledge and skills described in the school curriculum.

The second premise is that success yields confidence. This pervasive human trait is frequently missed in modern education programs that emphasize student differences rather than qualities that all students share. Regardless of their age, race, gender, economic status, or cultural background, students want to succeed and feel confident in their ability to learn. Success is the most powerful motivational device available to educators today. Students persist in activities at which they experience success, and they avoid, with passion, those activities at which they are not successful, or believe they cannot be. Students who experience success on learning tasks feel good about themselves and their ability to learn. They feel confident in learning situations and persist in challenging learning tasks because they believe their efforts will bring success.

The importance of incremental success has been recognized for decades by video game developers. Take, for example, Pac-Man, one of the earliest and most popular of all video games. When the Japanese arcade game manufacturer Namco Limited introduced Pac-Man in 1980, it became an overnight sensation. People of all ages throughout the world began playing the game, all vying to improve their scores. The goal of the game was simple: gobble up the dots in a maze while avoiding capture by ghosts. To this day, it remains one of the highest-grossing and best-selling video games ever developed, generating more than $15 billion in revenue.

Pac-Man's popularity is certainly not explained by the task. There is nothing inherently interesting about gobbling up dots. It also has nothing to do with cultural relevance or innate appeal. Pac-Man is equally popular among men and women, young and old, in countries throughout the entire world. Nor does it have anything to do with attaining a tangible reward. If you succeed in gobbling up all the dots in Pac-Man, your reward is to be presented with another game with more dots in a more complex maze and faster ghosts. That's like saying to a student, "If you solve these ten problems correctly, I'll give you ten more to do, and this time, they're going to be more difficult!" That's some reward!

Pac-Man is popular because players experience success on a challenging task. Every time you play the game, you have the chance to improve your score. When you succeed, you feel better about yourself, more confident, more assured, and better prepared for the next challenge. Most importantly, that success is based not on doing better than others, but on seeing your own progress and the pride you feel in becoming better.

The challenge for educators is similarly to ensure that students experience learning success. And just as it is true with video games, those successes don't have to be constant. Sometimes you fail. Even in Pac-Man, players get to "die" three times before the game ends. But those successes must come early, they need to be recognized, they need to be regular, and they need to be seen as the result of students' efforts.

The third premise is that students should have a major role in determining their success. According to Rick, this starts with helping students unlock three interconnected gifts: (1) a clear understanding of their learning targets, (2) access to information that allows them to monitor their learning progress, and (3) specific learning strategies that help them close the gap between where they are and what they want to achieve. Students who know how to unlock these gifts are more likely to feel in control of their learning success, take corrective action when needed to ensure greater success, and become more confident learners in any learning environment.

Based on these three premises, Rick then describes how to accomplish these noble goals in today's modern classrooms. But unlike so many other authors of current books about improving student learning, who are long on opinions but short on evidence, Rick writes from the unique perspective of a well-informed researcher who is also a highly skilled and experienced practitioner. Through personal stories of his own discouraging and confidence-building learning experiences, he describes his vision of "student-involved classroom assessment *for* learning" in practical ways that will make sense to teachers at all levels of education, school and district leaders, education policy makers, parents and families, and other school community members. He then goes on to outline how to structure "learning success teams," combining the knowledge, skills, and energy of these important stakeholders, in order to build educational programs that promote the individual well-being of *all* students.

I believe you will like this book for two reasons. First, there is a clarity and freshness about the insights Rick offers that will have you constantly saying, "Wow, I never thought about it in that way." But second and more importantly, you are likely to conclude each chapter saying, "I know we can do this!" What more could any dedicated educator ask of a book?

Thomas R. Guskey, PhD
Professor Emeritus
University of Kentucky

REFERENCE

Bloom, B. S. (1968). Learning for mastery. *Evaluation Comment* (UCLA-CSIEP), 1(2), 1–12.

About the Author

Rick Stiggins has devoted his professional life to understanding keys to student academic success in the classroom. His mission has been to help teachers, school leaders, policy makers, and school communities apply research-based policies and classroom practices that help all students experience the highest-possible levels of learning success.

His preparation to fulfill this mission began as a psychology major at the State University of New York at Plattsburgh, followed by doctoral studies in educational psychology at Michigan State University. Rick's focus on keys to student success was sharpened with early career experiences at the University of Minnesota, on the research staff of the Northwest Regional Educational Laboratory (NWREL) in Portland, Oregon, and as a visiting scholar at Stanford University. During this phase of his own development, Rick spent over a decade in classrooms with students and teachers researching and striving to understand (1) the task demands teachers face in managing the day-to-day classroom assessment process, and (2) how that process can positively impact students' motivation, actions, and achievement, as well as their sense of themselves as learners.

With this foundation of understanding in hand, Rick founded the Assessment Training Institute (ATI) in 1992 in Portland, a professional development company whose mission was to promote the "assessment literacy." He and his team developed and disseminated print, video, and online offerings that help educators, parents, and school communities in general learn to gather dependable evidence of student achievement and use that evidence effectively to develop truly effective instructional practices. Rick and the ATI team turned the spotlight onto the breakthrough practice of using "assessment *for* learning" or of engaging students in ongoing self-monitoring and management of their own growth while it is happening.

Primary among the materials Rick and his team created has been an award-winning professional text for teachers titled *An Introduction to Student-Involved Assessment for Learning*, now available in its seventh edition (Chappuis & Stiggins, 2017). In addition, he has authored numerous books, articles, and other writings on sound practice for pre- and in-service training, community outreach, and educational leadership that have helped literally hundreds of thousands of teachers, school leaders, and community leaders around the world improve their classroom practice, educational leadership capabilities, and professional confidence. Through these channels, it is safe to assume that Rick's work has impacted the learning and self-confidence of millions of students over the past forty years.

CHAPTER 1

The Dynamics of Confidence

"Optimism is the faith that leads to achievement; nothing can be done without hope."

—Helen Keller in Optimism *(1903)*

In this book, I delve deeply into a dynamic of American life that is almost never addressed in our public or private discourse about the rearing and education of our children. Yet this facet of early learning has a profound impact on each of us both in school and far beyond. I address the emotional dynamics of learner success and failure in the classroom and the impact of those dynamics on each learner's developing confidence or self-doubt. We all remember the constant evaluations we experienced in the classroom as well as at home. Sometimes those judgments were communicated privately while others became very public. Sometimes they were positive indications of success; sometimes they revealed that we fell short. Regardless, we always felt their emotional impact within, and, over time, those experiences shaped our beliefs in ourselves as learners. These are the dynamics that I examine herein.

As you will see, I begin this analysis by sharing the early successes and failures that shaped my learning life before, during, and after school. I share these experiences in the hope that they will trigger your memories, thus allowing us to develop a mutual understanding of how success, failure, confidence, and doubt affected our own lives. These understandings are critically important today because those dynamics continue to impact the lives of our children and because recent research on keys to effective teaching and learning has revealed ways to help every child attain the levels of success needed to grow into a confident lifelong learner.

In the presentation that follows, I invite all concerned about the well-being of our youth to team up and plan for the development of schools that raise generations of confident lifelong learners. I urge teachers and parents to team up with their students in a village-wide effort to build the confidence of every child. If our children are to be prepared to prosper in these times of rapid social, technological, and economic change, schools and families must take on the two-part mission of ensuring that *all children* (1) master the *knowledge and skills* needed to succeed in college or workplace training and (2) develop the *self-confidence* needed to meet whatever learning challenges life presents to them in school and beyond. The ideas I offer for accomplishing this and the stories I tell about the impact of those ideas constitute a practical exploration of how to place students in charge of their success both in the classroom and beyond as they face the learning challenges life presents.

THE ORIGINS OF CONFIDENCE AND SELF-DOUBT

Confidence is a very fragile emotion in a third grader, and, if it is lost, it can be very difficult to rekindle. This is graphically illustrated in the following story. In this case, the student's story is mine. This book is about how to keep learners from giving up in hopelessness as I did. As you read, take special note of how my thinking evolved over time and drove my judgments of myself.

Visualize little Ricky, a third grader at Canandaigua Elementary School, in Miss G.'s classroom where twenty-five of us are seated in straight rows and in alphabetical order. So, Eddie A. is at the head of the first row over by the windows. Next comes Jim B., then Judy C. Now, my name is Stiggins, so I am near the end of the last row away from the windows—way over by the bulletin boards. Dave W. is the only one behind me, and Terry S. sits right in front of me.

At reading time, Miss G. would instruct us to take out our reading books and open to a particular page of the story we were to read that day. She would turn to Eddie A. and nod—he knew his job was to rise from his desk, stand with proper posture, and read the first paragraph of the story aloud for all to hear. When he finished, Jim B. would follow, and so we would go down the rows.

Now, for reasons that we understand today but didn't back then, I have great difficulty with oral reading fluency. My eyes, brain, and mouth are not "wired" to work effectively together—a reality that has stayed with me but that I have accommodated as an adult. But back in third grade this was a very big problem. I was constantly embarrassing myself in a very public way. So, I needed a way to manage the risk—a way to minimize the embarrassment. The one I adopted was a strategy of fooling everyone into believing I could read (it's amazing how many people over the years have told me that they did this same thing). I would count the number of students in class that day, count down the same number of paragraphs to find mine, and practice reading it silently by myself. I found that, if I could spend a few minutes with my passage, I could almost memorize it and then stand beside my desk and smoothly recite it—no stammering, stumbling, or embarrassment.

However, as we were working down the rows taking turns reading, sometimes Miss G. would ask a comprehension question, and, if she happened to call on me to answer it, I wouldn't be able to—I wouldn't even know what the question was because I wasn't listening. I was practicing my passage. But Miss G. didn't know this. All she knew is that Rick was not getting this, and so she filed this evidence away for later consideration.

So back to class. As we proceed down the rows a paragraph at a time, Terry S. (right in front of me) is reading his paragraph. At that moment, the fear that is raging within me is profound because I'm next—sweaty-palm, heart-pounding stark terror. Seriously frightening . . . every time . . . not funny.

Terry finishes. Rick, you're on. As I am about to rise from my desk, Miss G. says, "Terry, you read that so well, and your paragraph was so short. Would you read another one for us?" Oh crap! I'm a dead duck! He reads my paragraph far better than I ever could have even with practice, and I am compelled to stand and try to read an unpracticed piece. During my reading, the anxiety overwhelms me. I can't think, let alone function. I'm embarrassing myself once again. My heart is about to explode from my chest.

Oh, and my worst nightmare was when Miss G. didn't ask us to take turns reading down the rows, but rather decided to do what I used to call "reading roulette"—where she would call on us at random to read. I knew I was going to get slammed, it was just a matter of time, and I was powerless to prevent it. What's the exact opposite of confident?

As I fumbled through the paragraph after Terry's, Miss G. would collect even more evidence of Rick's reading problem. She sent notes home to my parents informing them essentially that "Rick can't read." Now I was a good enough reader to read these notes, and I anticipated that a serious problem was brewing. At the next parent–teacher conference, Mom and Dad learned about the prospect of a failing grade in "Reading." Her purpose for sending this message was that it informed my family of my low achievement, and, when it comes to oral reading proficiency, it was not wrong. Also, it was supposed to be a motivator to get me to work harder so I could get a passing grade. It was supposed to be a kick in the pants (Dad took that part literally).

Mom, Dad, and Miss G. launched a frontal attack on Rick, the nonreader. "You have to try harder," they admonished. "We know you can do it if you just apply yourself." Nevertheless, my reading skills didn't improve, and, over time, a trend or trajectory of failure began to take control of me. It all seemed so inevitable—so hopeless—to me. And, you know, it has surprised me how many adults with whom I have worked over the years have told me they had the same experience.

As we continue with this story, please set aside Mom, Dad, and Miss G. for a moment. Center on me. The next crucial data-based educational decision was mine. At some point in the progression of fear, anxiety, and failures, I said to myself, "Rick, you're a nonreader.

It will always be so. Get over it." And I stopped trying. I gave up in futility. Do you think that was what Mom, Dad, and Miss G. wanted me to do? Of course not. They wanted just the opposite. So did I! I so wanted to read well—to not be humiliated anymore. I didn't know why I couldn't do it, but I know that it wasn't for a lack of desire. I was in a very real personal crisis, and just telling me to try harder made it worse.

There's another thing about my early reading experience that, as I look back at it, is both embarrassing and clarifying: From my first reading experiences in those early grades, the key lesson I learned was that good reading means you say each of the words that appear on the page aloud, smoothly and in proper order. It's a spoken thing. This was a scary thing for me because, right from the start, I missed words, stammered a lot, suffered public embar- rassment, and could find no way out. Nobody seemed to care about that part. They thought I was just being lazy. Reading seemed to be so easy and fun for my friends. They were always talking enthu- siastically about the books they were reading. This made no sense to me.

In those very early years, the thing I missed was that, when you read, there is something you're supposed to "get" from the text. I struggled so hard just trying to mentally process the words and say them properly that I had no mental wavelength left to think about the ideas hidden within those words, phrases, and passages. The mental process of comprehending literally escaped me. I didn't tune into "getting the meaning" until much later when I began to try to read the fishing stories in Field & Stream magazine. Yup, it's fishing to the rescue!

But even when I finally began to tune into "getting it," I struggled. Still, the challenge of mentally processing the text, even while reading silently, left little mental space to piece together the ideas within the text in a comprehension sense. It took me forever to read anything and follow the story. Reading in any form was a challenge for me in school, and in high school everything began to depend on reading ability. I was disarmed and hopeless.

When I got to high school, the testing and grading process almost immediately began to take its toll. It's important to remember that, back then, one assignment for high school faculty was to begin the process of sorting us out based on achievement. Anyway, I accepted my fate, gave up in hopelessness, and finished relatively low in the rank order of our senior class.

But back to the matter of emotional dynamics: Sure, my foundational problem always was reading difficulties. But in my thinking, I didn't leave it at that. I generalized from my reading problem to a much broader judgmental generalization that I was not wired to succeed in any facet of school. I gave up on learning as a whole. I accepted that it was hopeless for me regardless of the learning context.

Please make careful note of who the key decision maker was here—who was doing the judgmental thinking? It was me, and no one else.

As my classmates took entrance exams and applied to colleges, I didn't bother. What was the point? Why trigger even more embarrassment?

Later, I'll describe when and how my self-doubt and hopelessness were transformed into confidence. That, after all, is the very point of this book. But first, I want to establish why it has become essential today that we prevent such hopelessness from taking over the lives of any of our children.

THIS IS A CRITICAL EDUCATIONAL AND SOCIAL PRIORITY FOR MANY REASONS

Reason #1 is that, over the past two decades, programs of research conducted around the globe have revealed exciting new ways to revise the teaching and learning process in specific ways both to cause achievement to skyrocket and potentially to bring *all children* to a place where they regard themselves as confident and proficient lifelong learners in both cognitive and emotional terms (Black, 2013; Black & Wiliam, 1998a, 1998b; Wiliam et al., 2004). This book spotlights those breakthroughs. They center on students teaming up with their teachers to monitor, manage, and feel in control of their own growth.

One colleague, Dylan Wiliam, a leading researcher in this space, has contended in print that consistent use of the new practices featured herein can help us quite literally double the rate of student growth in our schools (Wiliam et al., 2004). Given the profound slippage in achievement that has become apparent due to the COVID-19 pandemic, the power of these innovations to boost achievement is a very big deal. Our deepening understanding of these new practices can help us develop supercharged home, in-school, and adult learning environments.

Reason #2 is that we have experienced extremely rapid technological and social change in recent decades, this is likely to continue, and our schools must evolve if they are to prepare our children to handle even more rapid change coming down the road. For this reason, civic leaders are directing schools to fulfill a new social mission. It is critical that educators and members of school communities understand this evolution. Let's analyze it.

Historically, as mentioned earlier, one primary social mission of schools has been to begin the process of sorting us into the various segments of our social and economic system. The assessment and grading system served what might almost be thought of as little more than a triage function, ranking us based on achievement at the end of high school. In that system, those in the highest ranks carried their growing confidence off to college. The others either gave up on complete hopelessness and dropped out or lost confidence, stayed in school, and accepted low ranks before ending their formal education.

However, early in the new millennium, civic leaders began to realize that there are certain lifelong learner proficiencies that have become absolutely essential for survival in our society because they form the foundation of healthy functioning adults. In response, the U.S. Department of Education directed educators to "leave no child behind" in terms of their mastery of these essential proficiencies. Later, schools were instructed to be sure "every student succeeds" in those terms. And now, society directs that "*every student* be made ready for college or workplace training." In other words, schools are charged with gearing *all students* up to thrive in times of rapid change. So now, educators are held accountable for delivering universal competence defined in these specific terms.

If schools are to deliver on this assignment, *we can no longer have any students giving up in hopelessness.* We must help *all* children believe in themselves, knowing they can succeed if they keep trying. This calls for a totally new set of emotional dynamics surrounding the evaluation of student progress. Regardless of their rate of attainment, children need to be academically self-confident—*all of them.* And the extremely good news is that we can do this, and I will describe how in the chapters that follow.

Further, as a society we face issues of racial inequality and equal educational opportunity. In that context, nothing is more important than making certain that all children come to believe in themselves regardless of their racial heritage or socioeconomic background. As we aspire to narrowing achievement gaps, we can and must come to see assessment not merely as a source of evidence of those gaps, but as an instructional tool capable of causing them to narrow. It can do both, and I will show you how.

Even further and in this same spirit, due to the COVID-19 pandemic, teachers are facing a much wider range of achievement in their classrooms than ever before because young learners have responded differentially well to remote learning and because home support for remote learning has varied immensely. Once again, to meet the classroom challenges of accommodating the wide-ranging individual differences in student achievement, of accommodating the unique demands of children with special needs, and of fulfilling the assigned mission of bringing all children to lifelong learner competence, we must seek to instill confidence and hope in them. This will require very strong and trusting student–teacher teams combined with parent–teacher partnerships as this team collaborates in the service of learning success. We have the tools in hand today to help each student find their own gifts.

This list of reasons why we must attend to the emotional dynamics of successful schooling goes on. For example, experts in developmental psychology have established the importance of early childhood education programs. One purpose of these emerging programs is to send children into kindergarten having already experienced some learning success, thus developing within them the emerging self-confidence needed to press on with their learning even when it's hard. For many early learners, initial contact with school can be scary. It can trigger anxiety, an enemy of successful learning. We need to help them see school as a safe place. Early successes can help with that. I will describe why and how as my presentation unfolds.

School psychologists have helped us understand that many adolescents are experiencing overwhelming emotional crises. Often, they have lost their way in school, within their families, and in their sense of their place in the world. It may be possible to remedy some of this doubt by helping these students learn how they can claim credit for their own academic success in the classroom. This is a strong confidence builder.

Referring once again to the impact of the pandemic, we know that increasing numbers of families have decided to homeschool their children. This relocation of the learning makes it critical that parents assume responsibility for building the academic confidence of their students. The research referenced earlier on how to build both academic success and confidence applies whether learning happens in school or at the dining room table. Parents, like teachers, are in a unique position to help their children to believe in themselves as lifelong learners.

All of these realities bring us to the critically important realization that, in these challenging times, our children, their parents, and their teachers need help in developing the whole child. The tenor of our times requires that they get that help. Local teachers and school leaders are fully aware of this. Parents see the effects of these crises first-hand, and many are desperate. We have arrived at a water-shed time in American education, a time when educators and their school communities must play critical roles in bringing our students successfully through this crisis. We have tactics and strategies ready to go to meet this challenge. Read on.

We know children don't all bring the same levels of learning desires or power to the schooling process. Further, we know all children don't receive the same levels of educational support from home and family. This reality has emerged with new clarity as schools worked through the remote learning experiences of the COVID-19 pandemic. Students don't all learn at the same pace or attain the same levels of achievement. Further, we know their interests and aspirations vary widely as they ascend through the grades. So, the pathways they wish to pursue in their learning and, therefore, the learning targets that become important to them will diverge as they mature. *But in the midst of all this diversity and complexity, we can and must hold to the value that all children are entitled to believe in themselves as learners, because only then can they master lifelong learner skills needed to pursue their dreams with hope of success.* This book is about how to help all of them find the kind of motivation and belief in themselves to which they are entitled.

LEARNING SUCCESS TEAMS

For all of these reasons, I urge that we build learner success teams to include all who care about and share responsibility for learner academic success and self-confidence. This includes teachers, students, parents, local school leaders, and educational policy makers at all levels. I urge all players to join in a village-wide discussion about how best to fulfill our shared responsibilities for the development of student competence and confidence. The problem has been that, historically, the most critically important villagers have been left out of such discussions. More about this will follow. But for now, I invite all who care about effective schools and student well-being to gather here and think with me about the powerful heretofore untapped potential sources of learner success.

Learning success team captains must be parents and teachers *working in partnership*. I want (we need) you to be in charge because, of all the players addressed herein, you are best positioned to promote the individual well-being of children. You have the most investment in and commitment to the development of the emotional dynamics involved in helping students become confident, competent lifelong learners. Teachers and parents have the most extensive personal contact with children by far and, therefore, have the most frequent and powerful opportunities to impact the development of students' confidence in themselves as learners. If our children are to find and build on their gifts, it will be because of the help you offer them, teachers and parents. Throughout the book, I will include sections titled "Teacher–Parent Teamwork Suggestions" to assist you in taking charge.

Teachers, I realize that you will not be able to fulfill your role without the full support of your local school leaders. You need policy priorities and resources to address learning success and self-confidence goals. I will offer you concrete advice and assistance herein for bringing them onboard. I have reason to believe that they already are on our side. Further, I realize that you are constrained by educational policy and resource priorities at local, state, and federal levels. I will show you how you can take the lead in partnership with parents and local communities to align local and state educational policy with lifelong learner priorities.

Parents, I believe you are among those who have been left out of discussions of pathways to learning success. School communities of parents absolutely must communicate and demand what you know is best for your children. I will show you specifically how to become enthusiastic partners with teachers to lead the village-wide movement toward the development of confident, competent lifelong learners.

Now for the big surprise of this book: I want the learners to be members of the starting lineup of our own learning success teams. They, too, have been left out of discussions of keys to their own success. I want them to be active players working in the service of that success. It is time to share the keys to the kingdom of academic success with them. Those keys unlock three interconnected gifts that underpin long-term learning success and the development of academic self-confidence: (1) a clearer and more complete understanding than ever before of their own intended learning targets, (2) consistent access to information upon which learners continuously can monitor their own progress toward meeting those achievement expectations, and (3) specific learning strategies *they can use* as learners to take charge of closing the gap between where they are at any point in their learning and what they need ultimately to achieve.

These three gifts allow students to take charge of their own learning successes, to feel in control of those successes, to take corrective action when needed, and thus to become confident learners. They allow students to remain continuously aware of the current status of their own learning, literally watching learning happen within them and developing the confidence to face new challenges. If we don't define "lifelong learner skills" in these terms, I don't know how to define them!

Consistent reliance on the three keys listed earlier has led to profound gains in achievement in schools literally around the world, including many in America (Black, 2013; Black & Wiliam, 1998a, 1998b; Wiliam et al., 2004). They help children come to believe in themselves by helping them watch themselves improve academically from one day to the next. The cumulative positive self-awareness arising from this ongoing progression of small learning successes, mixed with immediate course corrections in their learning when needed, can build in students a strong belief in their own academic capabilities. By helping students know where they are headed, where they are now, and how they can close the gap between those, teachers can help their students initiate and maintain extended academic winning streaks.

HERE'S WHAT'S COMING

In the next chapter, I continue to rely on my own learner stories to define the emotional (confidence–doubt) dynamics of the learning process in richer detail. I share more stories from school, as well as from the military, college and graduate school, and my professional learning. I chronicle how the progression of my discouraging and confidence-building experiences influenced evolving thinking. My purpose in sharing in this way is to make these dynamics come alive for you in very real-life, sensible, and practical terms.

Further, in subsequent chapters I rely on additional stories from the classroom to illustrate key points I wish to make about effective instructional practices. These stories come from my experience or have been shared with me by teachers and professional colleagues. I have shared these stories in presentations and instructional programs throughout my entire career. They are here for you to share in promoting sound practice in your context.

In Chapter 3, I discuss that vision in terms of learning, assessment, and teaching practice that differ so fundamentally from what most of what we adults of today experienced in our schooling years. I label this vision "student-involved classroom assessment *for* learning" and link it to very practical classroom strategies that are backed by ongoing international research revealing gains in student confidence, motivation, engagement, and achievement.

Chapter 4 speaks to *teachers* because you are in the very best position to give students the gifts identified earlier. In your chapter, I urge you to develop a powerful new kind of relationship with your students—a partnership in which you share responsibility with your students for their learning success by bringing them into a rich self-monitoring process while they are learning. I ask you to offer students a new role in the classroom, that of partnering with you in managing their own success. When we use assessment *for* learning, everyone wins. Teachers, your chapter also includes specific advice on how to establish partnerships with your students' parents and the larger school community.

Chapter 5 offers parents and the school community at large powerful roles they must play in this student success initiative. It informs *parents* about the contributions they can make to the development of strong student–teacher relationships. This chapter, or at least the ideas offered therein, is perfect for sharing with local PTAs or into other channels. I ask parents to become members of their child's learning success team, supporting their learning success in concrete and specific ways. We know that our communities care deeply about student success. This chapter offers ways for them to make powerfully positive and constructive family contributions to their student's teacher–student partnership and learning success.

In Chapter 6, I describe why it is essential to add *local school and district leaders,* as well as *educational policy makers,* to the village team charged with developing a new and productive post-pandemic classroom assessment–learning environment. Teachers and parents, I enlist you as the diplomats who will bring them on board. Teachers, I will show you how to introduce these ideas to your building and district leadership in positive and product ways. Parents, please remember that you are the constituents of school board members and legislators. You can make demands of them, and they will be listening to you. This chapter details what you can demand of them.

As you will see in Chapter 6, we need local school district and building leaders to create balanced local school district assessment–instruction systems that allow a student–teacher monitoring partnership to flourish without abandoning accountability. School leaders are most likely to engage in this village-wide effort if they see that their faculties and parent communities have teamed up to encourage them to become involved. In this chapter, I explain what such a "balanced system" looks like, why it's crucial to the success of student–teacher–parent assessment teams, and precisely how to build such systems.

Further, if policy guides practice, we need sound policies that link the monitoring of student progress directly to teaching and learning as it unfolds day to day in the classroom—something that has been missing in our schools for decades. Annual accountability testing has not, indeed cannot, do this job. Those who set policy must come to understand that we have in hand today the depth of understanding needed to set far more productive policies than ever before, and I show you how to help them see what this means. They must see that we are in *desperate need of breakout policy leadership* here at local, state, and federal levels.

We are in a position today to give every learner the gift of confidence. In the chapters that follow, you will read about the unique contributions that each team member can contribute to the confidence and learning success of each student. The transformation in teaching and learning values and practices I call for will not be quick or easy. We confront headwinds coming from a very narrow, decades old, and deeply entrenched vision of assessment's role in effective schooling. But we have it within our power to blow past this long-standing historical school testing barrier with the potential for stunning results for all students.

Teacher–Parent Teamwork Suggestions

Please note: Beginning here and at the end of each chapter, I will offer ideas for specific ways parents and teachers can interact with each other, school leaders, policy makers, and the school community in general in ways that promote the development of student academic competence and confidence.

In addition, I identify resources for educators and policy makers who wish to form local learning teams for further professional development in support of sound classroom, school, or district

(Continued)

practices as defined herein. Be advised that royalties I receive from sale of these materials go to an endowment at Michigan State University that supports research on those practices.

1. Historically, our local communities have counted on state and federal education agencies to set policies and allocate resources in ways that maximize school quality. However, in this case I am advocating a different leadership model. I want you, teachers and parents, to take the lead in learning about, embracing, and implementing a bold new set of ideas proven to enhance school quality. To reach this goal, you will need to take the lead in making sure school leaders and policy makers learn about, embrace, and support implementation too. You will need to speak truth to power in this arena. You must decide if you will take on this challenge. This book provides the details you need to make that decision. Please talk together about this, teachers and parents, as you decide.

2. As the beginning step in the building of your team, I recommend that all local teacher–parent collaborations around my ideas begin with participants reading and discussing this book—in pairs or groups; in person or online. It conveys only commonsense ideas communicated in a welcoming, jargon-free voice. It has no political agenda. As you read and discuss, strive to establish the importance and potential value of those ideas for your local situation. Bring local building and school leaders into your collaboration if you wish. As the chapters unfold, I will describe why their involvement is essential, and I will share ways to welcome school leaders and policy makers into your team.

CHAPTER 2

Failure or Success, Confidence or Self-Doubt

"One important key to success is self-confidence. An important key to self-confidence is preparation."

—*Arthur Ashe*

For the past fifty years I have been working in the field of educational testing. Why, you might ask, would anyone spend a lifetime working with something that made everyone so apprehensive in school? Most of us are elated that we don't have to experience the anxiety of those tests in our adult life! Who hasn't awoken in a panic from that dream in which the final exam is tomorrow and you haven't been studying?! Obviously, this is a very emotional realm. Again, who builds a career there, and why?

I did, and for reasons related to that dream or at least to the emotions it triggers. As a result of personal experience and decades of professional study, I have come to believe that the testing process can do and has done more harm to or good for student learning success and self-confidence than any other facet of the schooling process. Here's why:

The ongoing evaluations we experience as part of the schooling process form the very crux of our sense of ourselves as learners; they reside at the heart of the confidence or doubt that we carry forward as we move on toward life's ongoing learning challenges. Low performance shakes our confidence and can give rise to doubt. Success offers encouragement and builds confidence. Depending on how we respond emotionally to our evaluation results, they can power us forward toward success or defeat us. Each student gets to decide which it will be for them in each classroom testing instance. That decision will be based on past learning success, and, paradoxically, their ongoing school success will depend on how they decide to respond. As it turns out, their teachers can help students respond in positive, productive ways regardless of their past record, allowing and encouraging them to power forward in their learning. This book is about how students and their teachers and parents can work as a team to maximize students' learning success, wise decision making, and confidence.

During my early schooling years, as I already have told you in Chapter 1, I endured some pretty embarrassing and even defeating testing experiences. They robbed me of my self-confidence as a reader and learner both in school and beyond. The thing is, students are still living through these same kinds of potentially damaging testing experiences every day. Here's my really big-deal point: In our society, we tend to believe that that's the way it's supposed to be! Hidden in plain sight is an almost universal belief that students won't be motivated to learn without the threat, intimidation, and anxiety of pending tests.

But hang on! Later in my learning life, I experienced other testing events that were used in different ways by my teachers. These weren't intended to intimidate. They were designed and used to help me—that is, to support my learning success. In fact, they did just that, helping me to learn more, better, and faster; they rekindled some of the confidence I had lost in myself as a learner. I'll share those stories too. They defy the aforementioned societal blind faith in the inherent power of the threat and intimidation of pending tests. These experiences aimed for an entirely different set of more positive, productive emotions surrounding my development as a learner. They became the *cause* of my learning success, not merely the measure of it.

I have spent my career trying to understand the differences between these two kinds of assessment experiences. Why are those two sets of emotional dynamics—threat and anxiety versus success and growing confidence—so different, and how does each relate to learning success? If I could answer this question, I told myself, then we might come to understand how to bring positive, productive, confidence-building practices into the classroom *for every student all the time.* Had it not been for those productive turnaround testing experiences early in my life, I would have missed out on life-changing experiences and opportunities.

Over the decades, my colleagues from around the world and I have worked diligently to deepen our collective understanding of this human side—the student side, the emotional side—of school testing. Among the most crucial insights to emerge from this work has been the realization that the use of day-to-day classroom assessments to instill confidence in students while they are learning is a far more powerful motivator than using the threat of pending tests to trigger anxiety, intimidation, and the fear of failure. Positive expectations trigger hope. Hope, in turn, gives the learner the optimism needed to invest what it takes to earn more academic success, even when it's really difficult. My intent in this book is to share the lessons we have learned about these dynamics *from the student's point of view.*

In essence, what we have learned is that *successful learning in any context is as much about emotion as it is about cognition.* Further, and in that same spirit, *good teaching is as much about managing student emotions as it is about managing instructional strategies.*

One very meaningful way for me to explain the emotions that accompany judgments of success or failure in school is to tell you how those dynamics played out for real in my learning life. My first experiences with these emotions came early, as in the case of my reading difficulties. So, let me continue my story from there. I will share more experiences from my childhood, my military training, college, graduate school, and even my professional life that have added to the depth of my understanding of those judgments. I hope my retelling will trigger memories about your schooling experiences. The emotions we experienced— positive or negative—are being experienced by every student in every classroom today.

The French philosopher Marcel Proust reminds us that "a voyage of discovery consists not only of seeking new landscapes but of seeing through new eyes." As it turns out, over those decades, I lived an astonishing voyage of discovery. The personal and professional landscapes I have seen and the new eyes through which I have learned to view them have yielded surprising insights. As a result, I see a future for our students that promises to help them face their fears, muster the hope needed to want to learn, take the risks of trying to learn even when it's difficult, move on in the face of unexpected setbacks, and build on their successes to find fulfillment. Come back with me now as we explore those emotional dynamics starting with my earliest learning years.

EARLY LEARNING IN FISHING SCHOOL

I grew up in the small city of Canandaigua on a beautiful lake in western New York State. It's 5:00 a.m. on a summer Saturday. I'm 5 years old. Dad's just "rousted" (his word for it) my big brother and me out of bed for a day of fishing in a boat on Canandaigua Lake, one of the Finger Lakes of my home state. Anyway, I am already awake, having tossed and turned most of the night. Who could sleep?

Mom recounted that I used to be so excited on those fishing mornings that I would be visibly shaking with anticipation. I inherited that passion from Dad. As it turns out, this gift of passion has extended far beyond fishing into all personal and professional corners of my life.

The first and perhaps most important thing I learned in the "fishing school" was the importance of optimism. An older angler friend named Granger reminded me that it's called "fishing" and not "catching" for a reason. Sometimes, he said, fish can be hard to find, let alone catch. That's when you have to concentrate on remaining optimistic, he taught. Even when it's tough out there on the water, you have to expect to succeed. If you lose hope, you might as well go home. He urged me to become a student of fishing, constantly picking up and actually taking notes on fishing tactics that worked. The more you learn about what works, Granger said, the easier it becomes to work through your bag of tricks to find that special something that works when you're not catching. This made sense to me: To learn about how to catch fish, I had actually to catch some! In this sense, success (forgive the pun) spawns even more success. This meant I would have to fish a lot to learn how to succeed! No problem there! Oh, and by the way, hidden in these early experiences was the realization that passion is necessary but certainly not sufficient for success. You have to be willing to do the work of learning too. If you've given up hope, Granger told me, you'll lose interest in doing that work.

Luckily, my teachers (Dad and Granger) helped me succeed enough in those early days that I stayed with it, learned a ton, and gained confidence. And the thing is, I came to love the process of trying to figure out how to catch fish on those tough days when they weren't biting. The more I succeeded in those days, the more confident I became. I came to believe I could succeed every time I left the dock. Little did I know I was learning critical life lessons back then, lessons about far more than fishing.

But these were lessons I began to learn as a munchkin in "fishing school." Then there was elementary school. It was hard for me to remain optimistic there—that is, to feel in control of my success—because I didn't experience much of it. I told you my reading story. I lost touch with Granger's wisdom. I didn't learn enough to learn how to learn. I didn't experience enough success to figure out what actually worked. Eventually, I lost all confidence as a learner in school. I lost hope. The consequences of my decision to give up trying were both troubling and long-lasting. Now let me tell you how my turnaround from failure and doubt began.

IN SEARCH OF CONFIDENCE

After a brief trade school experience followed by a few months of work in that field, I enlisted in the Air Force. Had to. I drew a low draft lottery number and so was headed into the military one way or another. So, Air Force it was, and I headed off to basic training in Texas—my first time away from home.

Little did I know that I was about to be shocked into adulthood, ready or not. As part of this transformation, I was about to discover that those early judgments that I had rendered about my mental prowess were wrong. As you read on, note how my Air Force technical trainers used the emotional dynamics of being evaluated to advance our confidence and learning success.

After completing basic training, I was ordered to proceed to aircraft mechanic school. This technical training program was divided into five segments. Segment one built our understanding of how airplane systems work— engines, electronics, hydraulics, avionics, airframe, and so on. On day one, they informed us that, after three weeks of intense instruction, we would have to pass a 100-item multiple-choice final exam (here we go!) to qualify to go on to segment two. They told us we would only get one shot at passing this test.

Now here was the big surprise: The instructors did something I had never seen before in school: They gave us a copy of the final exam that had just been taken by the previous class. They said our exam would include different test items but our final would cover the same range and kinds of material. They didn't keep the key learning targets a secret the way my high school teachers often had. No surprises and no excuses. No need to "psych out" the teacher. So, each day at the end of instruction, our last activity was to go into that previous exam on our own (not guided by an instructor) and dig out the test items that related to what we had studied that day. Then we would figure out the right answer to each test item and why the incorrect answers were wrong. This really helped us understand the material we were learning as well, in effect, as the learning expectations of our instructors. Besides, this process always helped us find out whatever we still needed to work on. It really did build our (my) confidence. Please remember what my teachers did with that old test here to keep me in touch with the intended learning targets. This is *huge* and will come up again as we proceed into the later chapters of this book.

In the end, we took that final exam, and I remember scoring near 100%. Two things were important about this: First, I had never before scored that high on any exam ever in any context my entire life. I was stunned.

Second, my classmates did well too. This was new. In high school if this happened, the teachers would have been accused of being too easy, of promoting grade inflation, and of giving too many easy A grades. But here's what we have to realize: Unlike high school, the Air Force is not seeking to rank students in order of mechanical ability by the end of training as high school did. The mission of our technical instructors was different. They needed *every one* of us to come to believe we really could fix airplanes! Pilots really want that too! They were counting on us to know what we were doing. Our instructors' mission was to keep us believing in ourselves, trying to learn, and succeeding at it. Their assignment was to produce universal competence. They delivered. The emotional dynamics were different here: Competence and confidence rule.

Does this sound anything like my Chapter 1 mention of federal educational policies calling for leaving no child behind, every student succeeding, and every student being ready for college or workplace training? Of course it does. Hold onto that thought. We will come back to it.

But back to my story: This little win during the first weeks of tech school lit a small flame of confidence in me that had not burned there previously.

With my foundation of airplane knowledge in hand, I went on to aircraft mechanic school segment two. This time we were to learn how to use our new knowledge to diagnose problems in airplane systems: Why is this engine not starting? Why is the propeller not working properly? Where are electrical shorts occurring in the instrument panel? These instructors had mocked up simulations of the various airplane systems in which they could make things go wrong, and our assignment was to learn how to find the problems so we could identify possible solutions. Once again on day one, they showed us specifically how to succeed. The instructors took turns triggering system problems for each other to diagnose and then thinking out loud through their own diagnostic process so we could see their reasoning. After three weeks of instruction, practice, and feedback, our final exam was to diagnose ten new problems we had not seen before. We had to diagnose seven of them correctly to pass. I got them all.

Two segments completed, and two surprising (to me) successes! I was on a little winning streak! My confidence flame burned a little brighter. The Air Force had scared me twice, first during very challenging basic training and second by sending me off to a really tough technical school. At this point, I began to feel that I might actually succeed here.

There is no need to continue with details of my Air Force training story. This kind of teaching leading to success leading directly to confidence building went on for the rest of the program. Clear learning targets were shared with us at the beginning of each segment, along with concrete examples of poor and good performance. Guided practice was continuous based on really helpful feedback (these guys were really good coaches!). Continuously unfolding self-assessments helped us stay on track as we learned. Tough but fair final exams ended each segment, showing very high rates of success for me and my teammates. These technical instructors were, and I'm sure still are, the very best.

At the end, I was riding a very real winning streak and, more importantly, felt a kind of control over my own ability to learn that I had never felt during my school years. The thing is, success early on began to build on itself as I grew. The building confidence within me formed a foundation from which to continue to face the risks as I pursued more wins. Success spawns more success. At some point, the occasional setback was no longer discouraging. It triggered determination to dip into my bag of tricks to find keys to success. (Thanks, Granger!)

Obviously, this was a transformational personal experience for me, as impactful as the frightening events of high school final exams and state examinations. But, this time, fear and anxiety as the motivator were replaced by instructional practices specifically designed to build confidence, pride, and growing competence. I was ready to head for the flight line and real airplanes and was darn proud of it.

As things turned out, this experience taught me lessons about truly effective teaching and learning in any educational context that would come into play again later in my career. But first, I had more schoolwork ahead of me if I was to continue to overcome doubt and develop self-confidence as a learner.

PUTTING CONFIDENCE TO WORK

After my military service, I decided to risk my admittedly fragile confidence as a learner in a tougher context: college. As one of my fishing buddies says, "You have to risk to win." OK, let's risk and see what happens: I enrolled for full-time study at the State University of New York (SUNY) at Plattsburgh.

I had no idea where this was going. Mostly, I think I wanted to test the limits of my new confidence. This represented a huge risk for me. I had succeeded in one context but was totally naïve about this new one. The two environments—military tech school and university—are so different. I know that aircraft maintenance school isn't rocket science (well, no, actually it is), but still, it wasn't academic, and so I went in on shaky ground.

I went into this knowing two things: First, this was going to require really hard work on my part. But in my thinking, I had worked really hard in Air Force tech school and succeeded. I was confident in my work ethic.

Second, I needed a really big win right away in college. If I failed early, my confidence would be shattered, and I would need to find a new life path. This represented high stakes for me. I had to sell my car to pay the first semester's tuition. So, it came down to succeed or hitchhike home.

There's a funny thing about confidence. We already have spoken of this: If you have lots of it as a result of past success, the occasional setback is not a problem. You just reload and power through. But if your confidence is thin, you may lack the inner reserves to keep going. It's just easier to give in and give up.

These things also are influenced by the stakes of failure. If you're strongly confident, you can take bigger risks—raise the stakes, if you will. But the combination of thin confidence and high stakes can make it harder to take the risk of trying—of taking on a challenge, let alone meeting it.

I went into Plattsburg with uncertainty bordering on doubt. I was ready to work but worried that my academic capabilities might not be strong enough to succeed—that is, to meet the expectations of these "professors." That was why I needed a strong win as fast as possible. I needed to earn the confidence needed to stay. That's the thing: Confidence doesn't just appear in our thinking as if by magic; you have to work hard enough to believe that you really earned it. To refer back to fishing school, I needed to do the work of trying to "catch" some successes to learn new insights about success.

My needed win came in one of my first classes, Experimental Psychology. We each were to conduct and report on an experiment. I chose a study of visual perception. I am going to share a few details of this experience because it was crucial for my success = confidence equation. In my thinking, if I failed at this, I was gone. High stakes . . .

My study was challenging to design, interesting to conduct, and offered interesting results for me, my classmates, and my professor. I studied an aspect of visual perception: the impact of the blind spot in the human eye where the optic nerve connects into the retina. This small spot has no light sensors. So, we should have a blank spot in our visual field. But we don't. As it turns out, our amazing human brain fills in our visual field for us by merging the images seen by both of our eyes at the same time. But enough of the details. Anyway, I got an A in my first big college assignment—a win when I needed it desperately. This was a huge boost for my shaky confidence. I cannot tell you how important this success was in my life. It was foundational. It always is for the doubtful learner.

From then on over the next three years, I was able to build an academic record and the foundation of confidence needed to proceed through ever-more-advanced studies. As graduation approached, my professors suggested that I investigate graduate studies in psychology. While I had never considered such a path and had no idea what it even meant, I really had come to love the learning. Honestly (and I really mean this), by the end I had stopped paying attention to the grades I was receiving. I was having a ball independent of that. I investigated the graduate school options, and, yup, here we go again: Success leads to confidence leads to willingness to take more risks. These emotional dynamics are real!

On departure from Plattsburgh, I spent a year strengthening my academic record by completing a master's degree in counseling psychology while teaching introductory psychology to the freshman class of Springfield College in Massachusetts. From there, I accepted a fellowship for doctoral studies in educational psychology at Michigan State University. Events of the next four years at MSU would form the foundation of my career.

This was the major leagues of academic pursuits, requiring performance at levels far beyond anything I even understood, let alone had attained. Once again doubt arose in my thinking: Do I really belong here? There was a counseling center available for students at MSU. I made an appointment. My helper asked an interesting question to begin with: What was it about you that allowed you to be successful up until now? On reflection, I found myself quoting the lessons taught to me by my old fishing buddy: his lessons about optimism, working hard, taking risks, building on success, learning how to succeed, and gaining confidence. As our conversation wound down, my counselor simply asked, "Do you think those lessons somehow deserted you while you were driving here?" Her simple point was that, if one has a record of success, then there is evidence upon which to stand to remain hopeful of the future. She suggested that I just give MSU a try and see what happens . . .

Hidden in plain sight behind this experience, I came to realize, is the fact that the absence of any evidence of past success leaves one with no basis for hope. I will return to this later.

We all have an inner voice, and, to succeed long-term, we need that voice continuously to speak to our strengths. Accumulate evidence of success and believe it. We need continuously to tell ourselves, "I've got this. I *am* in control here." It is as if the mere process of saying those things to ourselves sends a kind of energy out into the world in front of us that allows that world to line up before us in the service of our ongoing success. Does that sound crazy? For me, this paragraph represents the very heart of this book. Please read it again.

LEARNING ABOUT LEARNING

I am not going to go into the details of my MSU course-work, professors, or challenges and successes I experienced. I kept up just fine and even excelled some. I studied in the general field of educational psychology with areas of concentration in educational measurement (school testing) and the psychology of learning.

But what I do want to share are a few really important ideas I learned during my graduate studies. What follows are learning experiences that ultimately fed directly into the new pathways to student learning success that underpin the student success ideas that follow.

As part of my studies in the psychology of learning, I had the opportunity to study reading comprehension and how it works. As an aside, these lessons helped me understand the reading difficulties of my youth. But more importantly, they go to the matter of how reading comprehension and learning in general happen in the human brain. I'll show you what I learned about this, and then I will bring these ideas back to the very reason why I wrote this book. *I will show you how they underpin the emotional dynamics of helping all students believe in themselves as confident learners.*

To begin with, then, we can read with comprehension if, and only if, we bring two things to the table: First, we need to be able to decode the text (words and syntax) in order to lift the author's message from the page. Second, we must bring to the reading sufficient prior knowledge of the topic addressed by the author. In other words, we cannot comprehend text about something we do not already know something about. Both of these ingredients are essential.

Let me illustrate how they relate and what happens when one of them is missing. Please read the following paragraph to see if you can comprehend it.

For some it is highly unsettling to come into close contact with them. It is far worse to gain control over and deliberately inflict pain on them. The revulsion caused by this punishment is so strong that many will not take part in it at all. But there is one group of people who seem to revel in the contact and the punishment, as well as the rewards associated with both. Members of this group share modes of dress, talk, and deportment. Then there is another group of people who shun the whole enterprise—contact, punishment, and rewards alike. Members of this group are as varied as all humanity. But there also is a third group not previously mentioned for whose sake attention in this activity is undertaken. They too harm their victims, though they do so without intention of cruelty. They simply follow their own necessities. Theirs is the cruelest punishment of all. Sometimes, but not always, they themselves suffer as a result.

All done? Please stop and think for a minute. How did you do? Most people have trouble getting this. Let me explain a bit more about reading as a mental process to show you why it's difficult to comprehend.

Reading experts tell us that we each carry in our own brain mental versions of the world as we understand it— this is made up of our own complex memories, ideas, and thinking. As the reader, we lift the author's message from the page (we decode words and sentences) and, in our thinking, actively compare the author's message to our own mental version of the world as we understand it. If we get the author's message and can link it to what we know, we comprehend it. If we can't decode or don't have the proper background content knowledge, we can't compare the message to our worldview and see how they relate. In either case, as readers, we control what happens in our own thinking. Comprehension is an active mental construction of meaning we carry out as readers.

In the earlier paragraph, you easily decoded the text. There were no unfamiliar words or sentence structures. But because of the way it was written, I deprived you of the essential link to the necessary background prior knowledge. Because I removed all of the proper nouns, you had no way to link the text back to what you already know. I'm going to give you that link now, and, as you reread, the meaning of this paragraph will be completely clear to you. You are about to watch yourself actually engaged in the very act of comprehending text that you missed before;

that is, you will be constructing your own meaning in your brain. Ready? OK, this is a passage about using worms as bait for fishing. Please go back and reread.

How did you do this time? Better, I bet. As you processed the text this time, you were able to link the message to your own knowledge, visualizing what the author was talking about. Now you will understand why, for example, most of us can't read a book on nuclear physics with comprehension because we're lacking appropriate background knowledge. In the earlier illustration, you didn't get it because of the word trick I played on you. But in the real reading world, comprehension hinges not on word tricks but on whether we bring the actual appropriate prior knowledge to the reading.

Given this illustration of the mental act of comprehending reading material, here is an interesting insight: The way we all use our reading comprehension capabilities depends on why we are reading. Note again that you are in charge and control of the actual process of making the meaning in your own brain. For example, if we are reading an exciting novel for pleasure, we rely on our memory literally to visualize what's happening. This is what well-written and exciting "page turner" novels are all about. *But if we read for learning, we decide whether or how to change our existing mental versions of the world based on what the author is intending to teach us.* This is an actual mental construction you build as you study. You are in charge.

Hidden in this illustration of the psychology of reading is a major insight about learning itself: Just as reading comprehension is an active process in the thinking of the reader under the control of that reader, so too is all learning an active process in the thinking of the learner under the control of each learner. Let's think more about this.

Consider once again that thing I said about reading for learning; that is, we compare our mental versions of the world as we understand it to the author's message in the mental process of comprehending. As we read to learn, we change our understanding based on the new insights provided by the author as we read. Remember how I said that if we don't bring the appropriate prior knowledge to the text, then, in effect, the distance between our current understanding and the author's message will just be too far (if we lack appropriate prior knowledge), and we won't be able to "get it"? Well, this effect generalizes.

In any learning context, if I am the learner wanting to learn something new and my teacher makes the learning target appear to me to be within reach for me (not too much of a gap *in my opinion*), then I am likely to try and I probably will succeed at narrowing the gap—that is, at learning. But even if I want to learn it, yet I find the target to be a reach too far for me (a gap too wide), I am more likely to give up. *Note who gauges the gap and judges whether to keep trying here (who's in control of the likelihood of success). It is me, the learner.*

The important dynamic is my sense of whether to go for it or not is based on my own interpretation of my chances of learning success. If I have experienced success recently and my confidence cup is full, even if it's a stretch, I just might still take the risk, invest the energy, and go for it. But if I have failed recently or frequently over time, I may have lost confidence in my learning ability, and so I may give up more easily. The generalization here is that the decision to go for it or not turns, at least in part, on *my judgment* of chances of my success—my confidence.

One key to learning success is for teachers to keep learners believing that success is within reach for them. Keep their confidence up. Only then will they stay invested in their learning. The whole idea for those who teach or learn in any context is to manage the gap between old and new so as to maximize learning success. Success builds confidence in the learner and the inner reserves needed to continue to take the risk of trying.

This leads us to a really big-deal question: How might we keep students believing that success is within reach for them? How can we maintain their confidence? Remember how my Air Force instructors did it? They used an old exam to help us see the learning target from the start and to help us watch the gap closing between us and the learning target. They showed us how to self-assess as we were growing to create our own record of ongoing learning success to instill confidence that success is within reach. This left us feeling increasingly in control of the likelihood of our own learning success long-term. The foundation of all of this was our ongoing self-assessment of our learning as it was happening.

The best way to support productive learning is to promote and build on success. Catch more fish, and you learn how to succeed at it. Succeed more, and you come to believe in yourself—gain confidence. As confidence grows, so does effort. The bottom line here is that learning is not merely an intellectual experience. It is emotional as well.

EMOTIONAL DYNAMICS IN A NUTSHELL

In my studies of the emotions of success and failure, I found very helpful insights in the writings of Harvard Business School professor Rosabeth Moss Kanter, in her 2004 book *Confidence: How Winning Streaks and Losing Streaks Begin and End*. Professor Kanter observed the dynamics of winning and losing among prominent athletic teams and Fortune 500 corporations. I was stunned to see how her conclusions generalized to the context of schools and education. She speaks of confidence not as a fixed emotion but as evolving tendencies, patterns, or trajectories. In essence, success or failure can become a self-fulfilling prophecy. "Success makes it easier to view events in a positive light, to generate optimism . . . easier to aim high . . . easier to find the energy to work hard because it looks as if hard work will pay off" (Kanter, 2004, p. 29). In effect, success can give rise to (read: *cause*) even more success. On the other hand, she points out, "losing streaks begin in response to a sense of failure, and failure makes people feel out of control. It is just one more step to a pervasive sense of powerlessness, and powerlessness corrodes confidence" (Kanter, 2004, p. 97). This is exactly what happened to me as I struggled to learn to read.

These are very personal dynamics. Based on their own record of learning success (or the lack thereof) as reflected in their own interpretation of their assessment, students will approach new learning in any context somewhere along a continuum from very confident to very doubtful about the probability of their future learning success. If they come to the new learning challenge carrying extreme doubt, this thinking probably will lead them to a "why even try?" conclusion and obvious results. But, even if these struggling students muster the courage needed to try anyway, they may approach the new challenge under an umbrella of stress and anxiety, which, as we have established, are the enemies of learning and performance.

*The only way to turn these struggling students around is for them to experience what they regard as at least a small success that they can attribute to their own efforts. If this kind of success is not forthcoming for them, **they are doomed**.* Unavoidable failure triggers more hopelessness. However, if they quickly experience at least a mini-success, faint hope might emerge, leading to a little more investment and a bit more success. The result can be the opening of a possible pathway to success and a tinge of confidence. Optimism might grow in them. Practice might become more persistent. A winning streak might form, raising the likelihood they will withstand other setbacks on their way and ultimately achieve success. What was the foundation of this progress? Please answer.

On the other hand, if our learners approach new learning with confidence, they are likely to jump in with enthusiasm. Immediate and persistent effort is likely to lead to success, which reinforces confidence, risk-taking, strong effort, and even more success. Over time, these learners will build the inner reserves needed to power through unexpected setbacks. But if an unexpected failure is so strong as to crack their confidence and cause it to waver, as earlier, an immediate success that the learners feel is due to their own work can patch the crack. Their winning streak can continue. Again, I ask, what was the foundation of this progression? Please answer.

The question we are addressing together in this book is this: What could or should be the role of the classroom assessment process in instilling confidence or doubt? Should we merely think of testing in school as the dipstick used to judge success or failure at a particular point in time and, having judged, move on? Clearly, this has been our tradition in the winner-versus-loser, grading-for-sorting context: assessment for triage into the winner or loser column. Or might we weave assessment into the teaching and learning process as a continuous source of dependable evidence of strengths and areas in need of improvement so students and teachers can plan learning experiences needed to bring students to their desired levels of competence? Should assessment merely be thought of as measure of achievement, or might it also *be a cause* of that achievement—assessment *for* learning? As it turns out, it can serve both purposes. Let's discuss how.

Teacher–Parent Teamwork Suggestions

I recommend that team members reflect on, collect, and share your own stories from your experiences in school or those of your children or grandchildren that resulted in a loss or strengthening of confidence or that impacted student learning. Share your stories, looking for the general insights they offer. Carry your stories and insights forward for use in discussions involving others or in deliberations about actions to be taken. They will serve as valuable resources in helping school leaders and policy makers understand how and why to use assessment *for* learning.

CHAPTER 3

Classroom Assessment *for* Learner Confidence

"Self-confidence can be learned, practiced, and mastered—just like any other skill. Once you master it, everything in your life will change for the better."

—*Barrie Davenport*

U pon graduating from Michigan State University (MSU), the next important experience of my career was, in fact, in the very heart of the standardized testing realm in American education. For five years, I participated in the development of the tests that comprise the ACT Assessment, one of the nation's two major college admissions testing programs. These were and still are tests that exert profound influence on the academic lives of America's youth.

As my time at ACT unfolded, I became increasingly uncomfortable with the idea that a single Saturday morning's worth of multiple-choice tests could drive the educational decisions (a) of higher education institutions regarding who gains access to their halls of higher learning and (b) of young adults as they consider the optional pathways of their lives after high school. Part of my discomfort arose from the reality that these tests, in fact, come totally out of the blue. They are separate from students' high school experiences, and students know so little about them. These circumstances trigger truly intense anxiety that can interfere with performance for some students. So, to counter this effect, I proposed that ACT design and offer seminars or workshops intended to prepare students for this experience—to orient them for thoughtful preparation and thus allow them to gain control over their anxiety. However, the ACT position was that their mission is to provide a dispassionate third-party estimate of each student's achievement for comparison purposes in college admissions. The interventions I proposed were judged to be outside of the scope of the ACT mission. When ACT declined my proposal, I resigned.

A NEW VISION

As I contemplated my next career move based on my ACT experience, I decided to act on an awarenss that was born in me in graduate school at MSU and that had continued to grow since then: my discomfort with the fact that the measurement community nationwide of which I am a part had defined its discipline solely and completely around the development and use of large-scale annual standardized tests. While I acknowledged the importance of these tests, I regarded it as shortsighted to say the least to completely ignore the other 99.9% of the assessments that happen for students, those conducted day-to-day in the classroom by their teachers. My mission became clear. I would move the spotlight to the classroom where assessments truly can contribute to student learning success.

I joined the staff of a private research laboratory in Portland, Oregon, and spent the entire decade of the 1980s in schools and classrooms documenting the task demands teachers face in monitoring the day-to-day achievement of their students. This work culminated with a semester as a visiting scholar at Stanford University studying what other researchers around the world were thinking about the meaning of sound classroom assessment practice. My team and I found that the typical teacher spends a quarter to a third of their professional time engaged in assessment-related activities and, very often, their classroom assessments are of inferior quality because the vast majority of practicing American educators (teachers and their local leaders) have never been given the opportunity to learn about sound practices (Stiggins & Conklin, 1992).

But more importantly, our research gave us a precise picture of what teachers and their supervisors need to know and be able to do to gather dependable evidence of the achievement of their students. From there, we began to build professional development programs designed to help teachers become what we later came to call "assessment literate."

It was here that my sense of a totally new vision of how to link assessment, instruction, and student learning success began to crystallize. I left the research lab to create the Assessment Training Institute (ATI), a professional development firm whose mission was to help teachers and school leaders master the principles of sound classroom assessment practice. We focused our early professional learning programs on helping teachers to master the creation and effective use of high-quality classroom assessments—that is, to gather dependable evidence of student achievement. We taught them always to be clear about the following:

- Why they are assessing
- What it is they intend to assess
- How they would create good test items or exercises and scoring procedures
- How they would communicate assessment results effectively

These keys to quality underpinned our definition of assessment literacy. As it turned out, our definition was inappropriately narrow—it left out a critical dimension of sound classroom practice. Here's how we learned about our error:

Early in our ATI work, a Canadian colleague, Anne Davies, shared a book titled *Changing the View: Student-Led Parent*

Conferences, in which the author, Terri Austin (1994), literally rewrote the guidelines for communicating about student achievement by helping students prepare for and lead *their own student-led parent–teacher conferences*. In her book, Austin describes the changes in the emotional dynamics of her students as they assembled evidence of their achievement, prepared to share evidence of their growth with their parents, practiced their presentations with each other, conducted their own meetings, and debriefed the experience later. She reported that their anxiety was very high at first but then began to fade as they worked to prepare, practice, and improve their presentations. Their focus tightened, motivation increased, and confidence grew. In short, they succeeded in fulfilling their new responsibility.

Shortly after reading Austin's book, Doris Sperling, a teacher from Ann Arbor, Michigan, who had learned of our focus on classroom assessment, called me out of the blue to invite herself to ATI so she could share some immensely important ideas with us. She insisted that she absolutely had to talk to us. As it turns out, she was right. During her visit she explained how she was involving her elementary students in the ongoing assessment of their own learning success while they were still growing. She was full of examples of what she was doing and how it impacted her and her students. At first their anxiety heightened, but then it dissipated, their focus on learning tightened, motivation and effort increased, confidence grew, and learning began to accelerate. Her work aligned perfectly with Terri Austin's!

Immediately after that, I got wind of educators in British Columbia engaging students in self-assessment while they were learning to build their confidence, motivation, and learning success. One of them—it was Anne Davies again—invited me to join this community to explore a wide range of student-involved classroom assessment activities. These teachers and school leaders became my teachers. I could find no one in the United States working with this set of ideas.

I came to realize that merely teaching teachers to develop high-quality classroom assessments was a fool's errand unless and until they also learned to use those assessments to build student confidence and to benefit their learning. We immediately began to weave these new student-involved assessment ideas into our professional development programs at ATI.

It was as if all of the issues and priorities I had been thinking about, worrying about, and working on over the years were coming into alignment at the same time! Our ATI team was bringing matters of classroom assessment quality to the fore like never before, we were helping teachers learn to use classroom assessment as a teaching tool better than ever before, and we finally were able to link the emotional dynamics of classroom assessment to student confidence and learning success more completely than ever before! We labeled our ATI focus "student-centered classroom assessment."

Then came the final stunning breakthrough. A colleague whom I had met during my time at Stanford, Dean Mike Atkins, informed me of a new research report just published in the United Kingdom synthesizing two decades of international research revealing profoundly positive impacts on student achievement of engaging students in self-assessment during their learning (Black, 2013; Black & Wiliam, 1998a, 1998b). I delved into this work immediately. Magnificent! Now the student-centered classroom assessment practices that were making such common sense to us at ATI were backed by extensive research demonstrating their efficacy. The UK researchers labeled this practice the use of "assessment *for* learning." Perfect! We adopted their label immediately (giving them full credit) and made it the hallmark of our professional development programs.

Now let me show you how this works in the classroom by reimagining the teacher's role, the student's role, and the very nature of their relationship.

"ASSESSMENT FOR LEARNING" DEFINED

Classroom assessment *for* student learning turns a major part of the day-to-day assessment process into a teaching and learning experience that promotes continuous learning success. It makes students partners with their teachers in making instructional decisions that drive their success. In other words, it uses ongoing classroom assessment while the learning is underway to provide both students and teachers with the understandable information (assessment results) they can use immediately to plan what comes next in the learning. So, students become consumers of their own assessment results, tracking their progress and analyzing what needs to come next. They experience and understand their own progressive improvement over time. Learners continue to believe that success is within reach if they keep trying. This process can put them on winning streaks and keep them there.

Before defining this idea more completely, let me frame it in three important ways. First, let's be clear that the classroom assessment process also includes periodic assessments *of* learning to judge the sufficiency of student achievement given the teacher's expectations for grading purposes. But in between those events, when students are engaged in learning, student self-assessments can help them along. So, both assessments *of* and *for* learning are important when balanced appropriately. But when we're in assessment *for* learning mode, the gradebook remains closed. It's time for growing, not judging.

Second, let's keep in mind that the foundation of any assessment application, including assessment *for* learning, is reliance on quality assessments to gather dependable results. Remember the quality control guidelines I mentioned earlier? Teachers must always

- Know why they are assessing
- Know what it is they intend to assess
- Be ready to create good test items or exercises and scoring procedures
- Be able to communicate assessment results effectively

We do little good to engage students in self-assessments for learning or assessments for grading if the results misrepresent their current level of achievement. Dependable evidence is essential.

Third—*and this is foundational in the clear understanding of assessment for learning*—everyone involved with assessment *for* learning, especially students, must embrace the mindset that their ability to learn (intelligence, if you will) is not a rigidly fixed human characteristic. It is, in fact, a dynamic and changeable human characteristic. Carol Dweck (2007) explains why this is essential for confident ongoing learning success:

[For students who hold the mindset that their academic ability is cast in stone,] mistakes crack their self-confidence because they attribute errors to lack of ability, which they feel powerless to change. They avoid challenges because challenges make mistakes more likely and looking smart less so. [They] shun effort in the belief that having to work hard means they are dumb. [Students who] think intelligence is malleable and can be developed through education and hard work . . . attribute slipups to a lack of effort, not ability, [and] they can remedy them with more effort. Challenges are energizing, rather than intimidating; they offer opportunities to learn. (p. 2)

In assessment *for* learning classrooms, students become important players in the management of their own learning. Therefore, it is essential that they believe in themselves as able to correct whatever problems come up in their learning with concrete action on their part. They must see themselves as capable of intellectual growth. The assessment *for* learning process is designed to help them see themselves in this light.

The idea is not to eliminate occasional setbacks in learning progress, but rather to use them to advantage in identifying and overcoming areas in need of improvement—to use them as a source of insight and hope *in the thinking of the student.* The great Duke University basketball coach Mike Krzyzewski is quoted as saying, "The key to winning is not losing twice in a row." He meant lose once and fix it, and you can remain confident. Lose twice, and it can raise questions, crack confidence, and make recovery more difficult.

So, when a learner suffers a setback, the key is to get back to success as quickly as possible so as to maintain their confidence in their own capabilities. This is the emotional dynamic that continuous assessment *for* learning can support.

Assessment *for* learning asks teachers to share learning targets described in terms that students can understand so as to keep students informed about the trajectory of their learning as it is happening. Expectations are shared with students from the very beginning of their learning so they can watch themselves grow, remain constantly aware of what comes next in their learning, and believe that final learning success is within reach if they work for it. In this way, teachers become merchants of hope.

According to Australian researcher D. Royce Sadler (1998), the key is to make sure each student knows this at all times:

- Where they are headed in their learning
- Where they are now in relation to those expectations
- How they can close the gap between the two

Assessments *for* learning are not onetime events attached to the end of the teaching. Students become partners in the self-assessment process during the learning by, for example, collaborating with their teachers in evaluating samples of actual work for quality. This reveals to them how to build on strengths to overcome weaknesses. Ultimately, students can become capable of communicating with others about their own learning success by accumulating evidence of improvement over time in their growth portfolios that they share, for example, in student-led parent–teacher conferences.

When these kinds of assessment *for* learning practices play out as a matter of routine in classrooms, as mentioned previously, evidence gathered in research conducted around the world consistently reveals profound gains in student achievement that are directly attributable to improved classroom assessment practices.

In her book *Seven Strategies of Assessment for Learning*, my colleague Jan Chappuis (2015) has expanded Sadler's three keys into strategies teachers can rely on to be sure students remain informed. Those instructional tactics are listed as follows:

Where am I going?

> Strategy 1: Provide students with a clear understandable vision of learning targets from the beginning of the learning
>
> Strategy 2: Share examples of performance along the continuum from strong to weak work

Where am I now in relation to those expectations?

> Strategy 3: Offer regular descriptive feedback during the learning
>
> Strategy 4: Teach students to self-assess and set goals for next steps

How can I close the gap between the two?

> Strategy 5: Use evidence of student learning needs to determine next steps in teaching
>
> Strategy 6: Design focused instruction, followed by practice with feedback
>
> Strategy 7: Provide students with opportunities to track, reflect on, and communicate about their learning progress (Chappuis, 2015, p. 11)

As we proceed now into chapters written for each of the key players in the teaching and learning process, I will fill in practical details about the use of assessment *for* learning by providing stories shared by teachers of what it looks like in actual classroom practice. In doing so, I will point out the roles to be played by each player working alone and in teams to contribute to the development of each student's confidence and learning success. As we go, it will become crystal clear why and how it takes a village to make our schools truly effective.

Teacher–Parent Teamwork Suggestions

1. Discuss whether the ideas shared in this chapter make common sense to you. Are they making sense? Do they seem practical for the classroom? Is the basic idea of student involvement in monitoring their own growth as it is happening likely to offer the opportunity to improve students' confidence in themselves as learners?

2. Teachers, it has been my experience when interacting with teachers about assessment *for* learning that very often you and your colleagues already are implementing similar practices in your classrooms. If this is the case for you, share those experiences with each other and with parents. This builds confidence that the ideas have merit.

CHAPTER 4

Teachers as Our Team Leaders

"Through my education, I didn't just develop skills, I didn't just develop the ability to learn, but I developed confidence."

—*Michelle Obama*

A **special introductory note:** *Teachers, in this chapter, I introduce assessment for learning strategies that can fit into any classroom. However, due to the purpose and intended audiences of this book, the depth of my treatment of them is limited. At the end of the chapter, I will direct you to resources that provide far greater professional learning depth.*

As I mentioned in the previous chapter, the early classroom assessment research completed by Nancy Conklin and me revealed that the typical teacher spends a quarter to a third of their available professional time engaged in assessment-related activities (Stiggins & Conklin, 1992). It is our custom to associate these activities with the process of gathering evidence for grading. But I am contending that this process can do way more than merely feed into the assignment of grades. It also can be the direct cause of student learning. Used properly, it can positively impact learner confidence, motivation, effort, and, most importantly, actual learning. This chapter details how to tap that potential. It describes a collaboration between you and your students in which everyone wins. Then the next chapter details how you can partner with parents in practical ways that bring even greater success for learners.

We have established that assessment is the process of gathering information about student learning to inform instructional decisions and decision makers at many levels of the schooling process. If we ranked all of those assessment uses and users in terms of their importance for student well-being, you and I both know that the instructional decisions made by you day-to-day in the classroom top that list by a long shot. As it turns out, if you bring your students into self-monitoring processes while they are learning, you and your students can knock the achievement ball right out of the ballpark.

It is critical that you understand that the instructional decisions made by learners themselves based on their interpretation of their own assessment results also can contribute to school success. They rank right with you in terms of importance. For this reason, I suggest that you establish a special *instructional* role for your students, one that they have really never been called upon to play in the past. To illustrate this role, I am going to share a story about a student I know named Kim. As you read, notice how her emotions influenced the judgments she made about herself as a learner.

Kim, a third grader, arrives home from school one day with a long face and carrying a piece of paper. She has always been a cheerful, well-adjusted child. So clearly there is something wrong. Her mom asks her what's wrong. The little one says, "You're going to be mad." Mom asks why. Kim hands her the paper and, tearing up, proclaims, "I'm a horrible writer." The small sheet of paper contains Kim's writing—it's beginning writer stuff on wide lines. The writing fills about three quarters of the page. Mom asks what she was supposed to write about, and Kim responds, "Something or someone we loved." Kim had chosen to write about a kitty who had come to join their family but had to be returned to the farm due to allergies. This had been a sad family experience. She had quickly bonded with this adorable creature. Mom reads the story quickly and finds that it really isn't bad. Kim got events right and even captured some of her emotions in her writing.

But at the top of the page there appears a big red F. Mom asks why Kim got an F. Kim laments, "The teacher said I was supposed to fill the page with writing and I didn't do that, so I didn't follow instructions and I failed." Mom tries to explain that the F had nothing to do with the quality of her writing. She says she really likes her daughter's story. But all of this falls on deaf ears. Kim's negative thinking already is locked in. She takes the paper from Mom, places it on the kitchen table, and leaves the room saying in a very soft plaintive voice, "I'll never be a good writer anyway . . ."

Now clearly it is the case that use of the F as punishment for not following the directions is bad practice. But let's look past that for now and tune instead into the effect of the teacher's judgment of "failure" on our little learner. Kim used the grade to make a sweeping and, it appears, incorrect generalization about her performance capabilities. She gave in and gave up. Kim was the key decision maker here based on her interpretation of her assessment results. This third grader's confidence was fragile. The damage was done, and I can tell you that it took a long time to undo the resulting harm.

Now let's return to the story, and fast-forward to Kim in high school to see how her English teacher helped a confident writer rise from the ashes:

She's in Ms. Inoue's eleventh-grade English class. Her teacher wants them to learn to read and analyze literature and how to write a strong theme paper. Students have been given the assignment of reading two pieces of literature by the same author and either (1) developing a thematic question based on their reading and answering it with evidence from the reading or (2) making an assertion about the author and relying on the literature for evidence to defend their assertion.

So now the time Ms. Inoue had planned for students to select and read the literature has passed. Now her goal is to guide them into the writing of their theme paper.

She begins by giving them a copy of a theme paper to read, informing them in advance that it is poorly written. Their homework assignment is to return to class the next day ready to discuss what makes this paper as bad as it is. What's wrong? What's missing? What's done badly? Be specific.

The next day in class they analyze, evaluate, and identify the various problems with this work. Ms. Inoue lists them on a whiteboard as they talk.

Next, she gives them copies of a paper that is of outstanding quality with the same homework challenge. What makes it good? What are the keys to its effectiveness as writing?

The next day they brainstorm the strengths of the second paper. Again, the teacher serves as recorder, collecting a list of positive features next to yesterday's list of problems. Then she inquires: "Do these lists have anything in common?" Kim is beginning to get this. She's beginning to understand how to succeed here. "Are there things listed as positives in one and as negatives in the other?" Ms. Inoue asks. This discussion yields a long list of factors that seem important in both lists, like sentence quality, punctuation, ideas expressed, word choice, organization of ideas, and so on.

The following day, she leads them through what she calls a "boiling down" of the long list of features into a manageable number by combining things closely related to one another. Ultimately, they agree on five key, relatively independent elements that cover the truly important things, including sentence structure, organization, voice, and expression.

On the surface, Ms. Inoue appears to be turning the definition of the learning targets over to Kim and her classmates. But, in fact, she is a confident master of what it takes to write well, and she is bringing her students to the same level of understanding she possesses through discussion and inference. Then, having done this, as things proceed, she will help them fill in details about each of the agreed-upon keys. Here's how:

She divides the class into five teams of five and assigns each team one of the keys to theme paper quality with a two-part assignment: define their key and then draft a scale or continuum of quality for *their key. What does their assigned key to effective writing look like when it's done very well? What about when it's done poorly? And, how would you describe midrange performance? Their next assignment due by the end of the week is to be ready to present the results of their team's work (definition and evaluation scale) to the rest of the class for discussion and refinement.*

Next, teams take turns sharing their definitions and levels of quality, debating and refining the keys, and, in effect, both finalizing and learning (hopefully mastering) in advance the standards of quality that will guide and determine the quality of their writing. The result is five clear and agreed-upon definitions and performance continuums for the features of writing that can (1) guide their writing as they compose their paper, (2) guide their evaluation and revision of their work to make it better, and (3) guide Ms. Inoue's evaluations of their work when it's done. Every student receives a copy of those standards. Kim's thinking, "I've got this!"

Please note that this brainstorming discussion is carried out under the watchful leadership of an experienced and competent writer, Ms. Inoue. She is guiding her students to a clear understanding of the keys to their own success. Finally, note we're a few days into this project, and no one has written a word of their paper yet! But now everyone is really ready . . .

Next, Ms. Inoue directs Kim and her classmates to begin writing. They go to work identifying their theme or assertion, tapping the literature for supportive references as needed, and composing their papers. As they go, their teacher keeps reminding them to tune into the keys to their success. Further, she informs them that in-class and homework time can be spent sharing their evolving work with classmates and giving each other feedback on how to improve their paper. She even invites them to ask her specific questions about how to improve if they wish. This sharply focused interactive work goes on until the papers are done and submitted to Ms. Inoue for evaluation and grading. And throughout the process, Ms. Inoue continuously encourages students to keep their early drafts and to notice and communicate with each other about improvements in the quality of their work and in their confidence as writers.

Would you like to speculate on the quality of Kim's finished paper and the papers of her classmates? Probably pretty good, and the exciting thing is the students knew this when they turned them in. Further, from Ms. Inoue's point of view, clearly defensible grades can be assigned to each paper based on the agreed-upon rating scales developed in class. But, in a deeper sense, the benefits that resulted from this student–teacher collaboration extend far beyond the successful completion of one theme paper assignment. Kim was developing the ability to evaluate and produce good writing—a critical lifelong learner skill. Now she sees herself as a pretty good writer. This is the munchkin who contended in third grade, "I'll never be a good writer anyway . . . " She and her classmates gained confidence in themselves as managers of their own learning. This is "assessment *for* learning"—they knew how to assess and improve their work as it was unfolding.

STUDENT–TEACHER TEAMWORK IS THE KEY

This story illustrates the kind of collaboration I want teachers and learners to develop. Note that Ms. Inoue made the learning target clear from the beginning of the learning. No surprises, no excuses. No need to "psych out" the teacher. But more than that, she made it clear in student-friendly terms by leading Kim and her classmates to her vision of a "good theme paper" by having them evaluate and discuss the quality of real samples of work. These keys to quality would form the foundation of her evaluating and grading of the quality of their papers. As Kim was partnering with her teacher to understand the meaning of success, in effect, she was preparing to succeed.

When Ms. Inoue's students actually began writing their papers, they had the criteria for success clearly in mind and could compose accordingly. When they gave and received feedback for each other, it provided the basis for self-assessment as they revised and refined their work. If any of this self-assessment revealed a roadblock in some facet of their writing, Ms. Inoue was there to provide focused help. Each focused revision brought them closer to success as teamwork paid off.

I propose a partnership agreement between you and your students just like the one formed by Kim and her teacher. Here are the very simple terms of this partnership as you might share them with your students:

As your teacher, I promise to do everything possible to be sure that you are able to answer the following three questions at any time during your learning: (1) Where am I headed in my learning? (2) Where am I now in relation to that learning target? (3) How can I close the gap between the two? It is essential that you know the answers to all three questions at all times because those answers will guide two things: the actions you need to take toward success and the kind(s) of help you may need from me, your coach.

In effect, you and I will be creating a mutual agreement to share responsibility for your success. I will take the lead in being clear about the learning target in two ways from the beginning of the learning. One way is by defining success using student-friendly language, and the other is by providing work samples that illustrate the range from poor- to good-quality work. Further, I will provide evidence from an assessment for learning early on so you can gauge the gap between where you are now and where you need to be in the end. Finally, I will be your coach as you take responsibility for doing the work required to close that gap and hit that learning target. As this process unfolds over time, you will need interim self-assessments to watch that gap narrowing, and I will make sure you have them. To the extent that you and I each fulfill our agreed-upon responsibilities, we both win.

The big idea here is to build your confidence along with your learning success. The process just outlined has the effect of eliminating the kind of uncertainty that gives rise to anxiety, the enemy of learning. As learners, when we see the target from the outset and see ourselves coming ever closer to it, we are able to remain hopeful—that is, able

(Continued)

(Continued)

to take the risk of continuing to try. We're always able to say, "I've got this." Further, if we experience an unexpected setback as we go, we always will have ways of dealing with it and getting back on track.

Let me conclude with one piece of advice: Confidence in yourself as a learner doesn't just happen spontaneously. It doesn't just appear as if by magic. It has to be earned. You must build it in your own thinking over time using building blocks of risk-taking, hard work, and success. I will help you. Each success builds your confidence. Even if your performance is or has been disappointing, small steps of progress achieved in collaboration with me can provide you with evidence that you are getting better. As this process continues, we will save your evidence of ever-better work. Then you can stand on each success to reach the next one.

You know as well as I do that our tradition has been to use that grading process as a primary motivator to get students to do the work required for learning. If "grade seeking" works as a motivator that brings learning success for some students, that's fine. But my aspiration herein is to offer a source of motivation that can work for all students, not just those at the top of the rank order—that is, motivation that arises from the confidence resulting from consistent learning success, as well as from the good grades that result. I believe that can be done with consistent application of principles of assessment *for* learning, and, as I have said, I can back this assertion up with extensive international research on the impact on student achievement that can result from the consistent application of those principles. When students understand the learning to be achieved and when they get to watch themselves successfully progressing through that learning over time, the pursuit of success takes on a life of its own.

In the words of Stanford professor Albert Bandura (1994), Kim and her classmates strengthened their sense of "self-efficacy." In the two paragraphs that follow, Bandura describes the anchor points of a continuum of this emotional dynamic. Clearly, consistent application of principles of assessment *for* learning can move students boldly toward the positive productive end:

A strong sense of efficacy enhances human accomplishment and personal well-being in many ways. People with high assurance in their capabilities approach difficult tasks as challenges to be mastered rather than as threats to be avoided. Such an efficacious outlook fosters intrinsic interest and deep engrossment in activities. They set themselves challenging goals and maintain strong commitment to them. They heighten and sustain their efforts in the face of failure. They quickly recover their sense of efficacy after failures or setbacks. They attribute failure to insufficient effort or deficient knowledge and skills which are acquirable. They approach threatening situations with assurance that they can exercise control over them. Such an efficacious outlook produces personal accomplishments, reduces stress and lowers vulnerability.

In contrast, people who doubt their capabilities shy away from difficult tasks which they view as personal threats. They have low aspirations and weak commitment to the goals they choose to pursue. When faced with difficult tasks, they dwell on their personal deficiencies, on the obstacles they will encounter, and all kinds of adverse outcomes rather than concentrate on how to perform successfully. They slacken their efforts and give up quickly in the face of difficulties. They are slow to recover their sense of efficacy following failure or setbacks. Because they view insufficient performance as deficient aptitude it does not require much failure for them to lose faith in their capabilities. (Bandura, 1994, p. 71)

We help students progress toward ever-stronger self-efficacy and academic success, first by helping them understand what good work looks like, and second by using ongoing self-monitoring to help them track their own progress and thus come to believe that ultimate success is within reach for them. The contract I envision between teacher and student is one in which, as a team, you engage in interpreting the evidence of each assessment and continuously deciding what comes next in the learning. As long as they are making progress and feel that their work is the reason why, students will become more and more confident in themselves as able learners.

Think with me for a moment about struggling students. I have contrasted these students to confident, successful students in Table 4.1. Please take a moment to study the contrast in emotional dynamics for these students. Assessment *for* learning is especially important for those who struggle. Often, the gap between your expectations and their current status is wide—both in reality and in *their* minds. They need to experience a baby step of success in their learning to light that small flame of success that I experienced in my Air Force technical training. It will only take a few of those to help them begin to feel in control. I can tell you from my personal experience that, if we just prime their pump with these kinds of (for them) unexpected successes, they will go on internal control and start flying on their own. They just need (I just needed) help from launch control.

TABLE 4.1 ● Contrasting Dynamics of the Assessment Experiences

STUDENTS WHO ARE SUCCEEDING	STUDENTS WHO ARE STRUGGLING
Assessments provide:	
Continuous evidence of success	Continuous evidence of failure
Likely effect on the learner:	
Hope rules; remain optimistic	Hopelessness dominates
What the student is probably thinking in the face of results:	
It's all good; I'm doing fine	This hurts me; I'm not safe here
See the trend? I succeed as usual	I never get it
I want more success	I just want one success
We focus on what I do well	Why is it always about what I *can't* do?
I know what to do next	I'm lost

STUDENTS WHO ARE SUCCEEDING	STUDENTS WHO ARE STRUGGLING
Move on, grow, learn new stuff	Defend, hide, get away from here
Feedback helps me	Feedback never helps—don't know what it means
Public success feels very good	I don't belong here
Actions likely to be taken by the learner:	
Take risks—stretch, go for it!	Trying is too dangerous—retreat, escape
Seek what is new and exciting	Can't keep up—can't handle new stuff
Seek challenges	Seek what's easy
Practice with gusto	Don't practice
Persist	Give up
Likely result of these actions:	
Lay foundations now for success later	Can't master prerequisites needed later
Success becomes *the* reward	No success = no reward
Self-enhancement	Self-defeat
Positive self-fulfilling prophecy	Negative self-fulfilling prophecy
Extend the effort in face of difficulty	Give up quickly in face of difficulty
Acceptance of responsibility	Denial of responsibility
Make success public	Cover up failure (e.g., cheat)
Self-analysis tells me how to win	Self-criticism is easy given my record
Manageable stress	Always high stress

(Continued)

(Continued)

STUDENTS WHO ARE SUCCEEDING	STUDENTS WHO ARE STRUGGLING
Curiosity, enthusiasm	Boredom, frustration, fear
Resilience	Yielding quickly to defeat
Continuous adaptation	Inability to adapt

Source: Stiggins, R. (2014). *Revolutionize assessment: Engage students, inspire learning.* Corwin.

OPPORTUNITIES TO ASSESS FOR LEARNING

Let's consider specific places and ways a teacher might bring students into the assessment *for* learning process. The stories I have offered so far illustrate some of the opportunities. In this section, I offer a few more concrete ways to bring students into classroom self-monitoring to enhance their learning success. Please understand that these suggestions represent just a few of a wonderous array of strategies and tactics available for student engagement. Additional professional learning resources are annotated at the end of the chapter for those who wish to explore and practice with these ideas in greater depth.

All who presume to monitor student learning must begin with the following:

1. A clear sense of *why they will monitor* student learning

2. A clear and complete vision of the *learning target(s)* to be mastered; what will we monitor?

3. Skill in gathering *dependable evidence* of student mastery of those learning target(s)

4. Plans for *effectively communicating* the results to the intended user(s) in a timely and understandable form

Each of these offers concrete and specific opportunities for welcoming students in their own teaching and learning process while they are growing.

1. CLEAR PURPOSE

The reason for assessing is clear when, and only when, all involved know who is going to use the results to inform specific instructional decision(s). In that regard, we can monitor to (a) support student learning or (b) judge its sufficiency. In the latter case, we compare student achievement to expectations and, for example, assign report card grades.

When the purpose is to support student learning, we monitor to determine where students are now in their learning so we can determine what comes next in their learning. Both teachers and their students can come to know these things if they collaborate in monitoring learning progress while it's happening. By engaging learners in such self-monitoring, we can keep them continuously informed about the answers to their own three assessment *for* learning questions: Where am I headed in my learning? Where am I now? And how can I close the gap between the two? By answering these questions, we help students manage the gap so it doesn't look too big and overwhelm them. We maintain confidence. Their confidence.

Also, note where the locus of control over learning success resides when we frame the assessment *for* learning questions in the first-person singular. Students become partners in managing the journey to their own success. They can begin to anticipate, on their own, what comes next in their learning. From there they may be able to set new goals for their own learning. This can contribute to the development of their sense of control over their own learning success and their confidence as lifelong learners.

2. CLEAR LEARNING TARGETS

Students are most likely to succeed in hitting learning targets when three conditions are satisfied: They (1) see and understand the target, (2) value the target as something they want to master, and (3) feel confident that they can do so if they try.

Regarding the first condition, students can hit any target that they can see and that holds still for them. But if those expectations are not clear and they are left to guess, they won't be able to see their gap, let alone contribute to closing it. This means that it is essential that we inform students about the targets up front in student-friendly terms they can understand. It's also helpful if we share samples of work spanning the range from poor to good quality. Learning targets shared in these ways contribute to the development of optimism in learners that they can succeed if they invest. It is a confidence builder in the face of risk.

When it comes to helping students value the learning targets, I must leave this one to you with your content expertise and experience in making targets relevant to your students. But I will offer one suggestion about making learning targets valuable in the minds of students: It is surprising how valuable a learning target can become once students realize that they probably can master it when, previously, they didn't have that confidence. The student-involved assessment *for* learning process as described herein is designed to make learning targets appear to be within reach. This is why it is a confidence builder.

So, in effect, once students satisfy the first two conditions, they have laid the groundwork for bringing them closer to the third key, the belief that success is within reach if they go for it. We can seal that deal for them by using the ongoing self-assessment process to help them watch themselves gaining ground on the finish line. This brings hope, optimism, and practice in the direction of success.

Here is an important underlying assessment *for* learning perspective: Regardless of the nature of any particular learning target or how it is most effectively mastered, time passes while learning is happening. Confidence comes to learners when they get to know up front what is about to change in them as they learn and if we help them literally watch those changes happening for them. A sense of control over their well-being happens for them when they see how their learning actions pay off with real growth in their own capabilities. It doesn't have to be immense growth. It can be very small. But it is their win due to their own efforts. We know how to give them that control and confidence.

3. QUALITY ASSESSMENT

The benefits of instructional decisions made by students and teachers will be only as strong as the dependability of the evidence upon which the decisions are based—that is, on the quality of the assessments used. High-quality assessments arise from and promise to serve a clear purpose, accurately reflect the intended learning target, rely on quality test exercises and scoring guides, and communicate results effectively. Professional development guides are identified at the end of the chapter that offer in-depth training on these standards of quality. But I do want to mention two ways to use classroom tests as teaching and learning tools that promote greater student learning success.

One idea familiar to all of us is to use them as pretests, giving you information about how and where to start instruction and giving students an advanced vision of where they're headed in their learning. It can be helpful to score the test and analyze results with students as partners to begin to give them a sense of the nature of their strengths to build on and gaps to be closed. In this case, it is important to protect the privacy of each student's results to prevent embarrassment, which can harm confidence.

Another idea is practice assessments used during the learning to help students track their growth. This can help them identify strengths to build on and areas in need of more work. Remember from Chapter 2 my story of Air Force tech school where instructors gave us a copy of the final exam taken by the previous class? Our final would include different test items but would cover the same material. We were able to use it on a daily basis to identify areas in need of improvement and to support our learning by analyzing right and wrong answers. It was a teaching and learning tool. Once again, this is a confidence builder.

A variation on this idea is to engage students actually in building their own practice assessments. The process of writing test items can take them right inside the important learning. And the process of developing practice scoring guides for essay or performance assessments does the same. These kinds of practices can bring students to places where they can say, "I am not there yet, but I'm growing ever closer and I will succeed if I invest. I'm in control here."

4. EFFECTIVE COMMUNICATION

The best-quality assessment ever created is wasted if the results are miscommunicated to the intended user. Nowhere is that perspective more important than in an assessment *for* learning classroom. Assessment results can support student growth only if they describe attributes of student work in terms the learner understands and can act upon in order to improve. Results need to describe attributes of student work and reveal to the student in concrete terms how to do better next time. So, obviously, they need to be used in classrooms in which it is OK not to be good at the learning material to begin with—there needs to be an ongoing sequence of "next times." This chain of back-and-forth communication must happen during the learning.

Continuous access to descriptive feedback as they learn can help students see how and believe that their actions lead to better-quality work. Result? A growing sense of academic self-efficacy. Without this feedback, they have no way to judge the impact of their actions. Result? Vulnerability. Uncertainty can cause occasional setbacks to become losing streaks and hopelessness. All of this is preventable. Descriptive feedback effectively delivered during learning can show students that gaps in that learning are narrowing due to actions on their part. This is all about building confidence.

Further, students can be communicators of their own progress and success in hitting learning targets. If they are clear about the targets and have developed the understanding and vocabulary needed to talk about them, and if they are given the opportunity to collect dependable evidence of their own success over time, they are in a position to inform themselves and others of their own progress. For example, they can share their progress with classmates and receive feedback on how to do better next time. Student-to-student feedback supports learning effectively too, both in terms of helping the recipient learn how to improve and in terms of improving the giver's thinking about keys to their own learning success. When students see the learning target and have the vocabulary needed to communicate about it, they are prepared to ask their teachers for the help they need to succeed. And, of course, all of this prepares students to be able to share the evidence of their growth and learning success with their parents.

In fact, I have a story to share about students telling their own stories in student-led parent–teacher conferences, which I believe to be the biggest breakthrough in communicating about student achievement in the past century. This story came to me from my Canadian colleague—yes, it was Anne D. again—one of my teachers in the realm of assessment *for* learning.

Ms. Murphy had committed to engaging her students as partners in telling the story of their own growth by replacing traditional parent–teacher conferences with student success conferences. She had prepared her students for success very carefully over an extended period of time by doing all of the following:

- *Basing her instruction on very clear learning targets, which she shared with students from the outset of instruction*

- *Developing high-quality assessments of those targets*

- *Engaging students in ongoing self-assessment as they learned, helping them not only to understand the learning targets but also to develop the vocabulary needed to tell the story of their growth*

- *Having each student build a growth portfolio full of examples of their work as it changed over time to present to and discuss with parents*

- Giving students class time to practice their conference presentations with one another, which not only helped them improve their presentation skills but also prompted them to reflect further on their learning gains

The student success conferences were scheduled for the late afternoon and staggered so that there were three or four families meeting in the classroom at a time. Students welcomed their family members as they arrived, introduced them to Ms. Murphy, retrieved their portfolios from the file, and ushered their family to a designated table, where they gave their presentations, shared their work and its results, and discussed their progress with their families. Ms. Murphy circulated among the tables, contributing as needed.

As she walked by one table, she was surprised to hear a student conducting his conference in Spanish. He had not practiced this way, but all involved—his mom, dad, grandmother, and younger sibling—were paying rapt attention. Although Ms. Murphy didn't speak Spanish herself, she could see that this student was proceeding through his growth portfolio, sharing the learning targets, and describing his successes and challenges with actual examples of his work. At the end of his presentation, his family applauded.

As they were leaving, Ms. Murphy met them at the door and thanked them for coming. Last to leave was Grandma, who simply clasped Ms. Murphy's hand with tears in her eyes and said "thank you" in English. When they were gone, Ms. Murphy commented to her student on his use of Spanish and asked him how the conference had gone. The student replied that when his family talks about really important things and Grandma is there, they do so in Spanish to include and honor her. The family meeting had gone very well, he said. Ms. Murphy could see that. She could see how proud his family was and that he felt immensely successful.

This, I submit, can be truly effective communication of student learning progress, and so it represents a good summary of the ideas offered in this chapter. In this case, everyone involved understood the meaning of academic success. It was OK for students not to be good at hitting the targets at the beginning of instruction because they were just getting started. Ms. Murphy helped them understand the learning targets they needed to hit. All involved were partners in the accumulation of and reflections on evidence of changes in performance over time as collected in students' growth portfolios.

Students came to their success conferences with an understanding of both the targets and the vocabulary needed to talk about them with their families. But the real pride for the students came from knowing they had grown and being able to prove it to all who asked. They were strong and confident.

And clearly, this method of sharing successes accommodates diverse family cultures.

I have watched parents quite literally be moved to tears with pride and surprise at the learning and confidence their children demonstrated in such conferences and the maturity with which they conducted their meeting.

Teachers, you will have great difficulty developing and sustaining a classroom oriented toward academic success and student confidence working alone. Your students can handle some of the workload with enthusiasm if given the opportunity and preparation. Further, their parents can join the team too. The next chapter spells out parents' potential contributions to student growth in concrete terms. As you will see, I urge them to partner with you in the service of this mission. I urge you to reach out to the local community to let them know what is possible in the promotion of student success and confidence to enlist their support and action on your behalf.

In fact, this idea of community-based, student-involved, and student-growth-oriented assessment plays a prominent role in the principles of sound classroom practice recently advanced by the National Education Association (NEA) Task Force on the Future of Assessment (2022). Their principles call for providing educators with opportunities to develop their assessment literacy so they can inspire learning, make appropriate instructional decisions, and give students the opportunity to demonstrate their knowledge, creativity, and skills. These Task Force principles are listed in detail in the Appendix.

Teacher–Parent Teamwork Suggestions

1. Identify students you know who are at each end of Bandura's self-efficacy continuum. How do those children think differently about themselves and act differently in the classroom? What might it take to move students along toward the positive end of that continuum?

2. Think about how parents and teachers might work together to give student success conferences with parents a try. What would be the focus of such conferences—to talk about something? What preparation would be needed both to prepare students to tell their own story and to organize for the conferences to take place? What might it take to convince school leaders that it's a good idea to give them a try?

3. Teachers, if you wish to learn more about specifically how to make assessment *for* learning operational in your classroom, turn to the following two professional learning guides. These guides rely on local learning team-based professional development strategies that rely heavily on learning through classroom practice. They contain many true stories from the classroom that parents will find enlightening too:

-   Chappuis, J. (2015). *Seven strategies of assessment* for *learning* (2nd ed.). Pearson.

    Offers dozens of examples of assessment *for* learning at work in the classroom.

- Chappuis, J., & Stiggins, R. (2020). Classroom assessment for student learning: Doing it right, using it well (3rd ed.). Pearson.

  Practicing classroom teachers learn to engage their students in self-monitoring while they are learning to develop their academic competence and confidence. Relies on local learning teams to permit teachers to grow together.

CHAPTER 5

Guidelines for Parents

"With confidence, you can reach truly amazing heights; without confidence, even the simplest accomplishments are beyond your grasp."

—Jim Loehr

The future of our rapidly evolving society turns on our ability to produce generations of competent, confident lifelong learners. Parents, I am contending that success in doing so will require that we establish strong student–teacher partnerships that provide opportunities for learners to watch themselves learn and grow. The result can be rapid academic growth and the promotion of self-confidence in school. In this chapter, I suggest several specific ways you can support your child's academic competence and confidence, erasing any doubts they may hold about their academic capabilities as they travel their schooling journey.

Over the past few decades, just as breakthroughs in the fields of medicine, computer technology, and energy production, for example, have yielded exciting and productive solutions to the problems we face, so too have educational researchers teamed up around the world to discover far better ways to promote student learning success and self-confidence. As you have seen in previous chapters, they have uncovered productive new ways to engage students in monitoring their own growth and in taking responsibility for and control of their own learning success. In our rapidly changing world and as your students mature, they will need to be lifelong learners. You can team up with local schools to make sure they're ready. Here are some silver lining plays that you can rely on as you team up with your local teachers in the service of this goal:

GUIDELINE 1: BE AN ACTIVE PLAYER FOR YOUR CHILDREN AND THEIR TEACHERS

We have established that we want (indeed, need) to set students up to become effective managers of their own learning by making sure they are always in touch with their answers to three driving questions: Where am I headed in my learning? Where am I now relative to those expectations? How can I close the gap between the two? These questions also can provide a consistent focus for your conversations with your student about school. They go far beyond traditional home/family questions—for example, what did you learn in school today? Or, how did you do in school? Or, did you do your homework?

Here are some in-home versions of those three driving questions that let your child know *that you believe in them*— this is very important: What are you trying to learn? Ask them to show you and talk with you about some samples of their work, being sure to advise them that you know they're still learning so they may not be good at it yet. That's OK. Sit with them and listen. Maybe talk about your experience in learning the same kinds of stuff.

Ask them if they see themselves getting better at it over time. How do they know? Maybe they could show you where they used to be when they first started and where they are now. Ask them to describe what has changed in their capabilities. What are their strengths? What kinds of improvements are they looking for? How is their teacher helping them figure these things out? Is there any way you can help? Talk to them.

Further, you can delve into what they think it's going to take for them to close the gap. How is their teacher helping? Are classmates helping each other? Tell them you're looking forward to seeing the final evidence that they succeeded whenever that happens.

In a more general sense, it's OK to ask your children a very focused question: What is it you need from your teacher to help you succeed? How can we or your teacher help you? Gently solicit truthful, honest answers. Please be advised that it is accepted practice to share the answers you receive with your child's teacher. They will welcome it with open arms.

The idea here is not necessarily to become the teacher (unless you are qualified to fulfill that role, of course) depending on the grade level and content being learned. But short of that, parents need to be actively engaged with their children about their real school stuff: their learning goals, progress to date, how they feel about the help they're getting, and so on. If you sense that there are things your student's teacher needs to know about, go to them and share what you have learned so you can discuss needed actions. Be an active player.

GUIDELINE 2: POSITIVE TALK

Every student goes off to school for the first time full of hope and optimism. They all really want to succeed and are excited to get started. Our challenge as parents and educators is to be sure they never lose that positive buoyancy. And if they do begin to slide, we must rally with them to overcome such setbacks as quickly as possible to get back to the plus side.

Positive thinking can become a self-fulfilling prophecy. If we face a challenge expecting to succeed in whatever terms, we will be more willing to invest what it takes to figure out how to win. When we embrace positive expectations, we send an energy out into the future that causes the world to line up in favor of our success. If this becomes a consistent pattern of our self-thought, over time we are more likely to begin to accumulate a record of successes along with the bag of tricks we can tap into for the rest of our life. If that is not the definition of a lifelong learner, I don't know how to define it!

One excellent way for us parents to support optimism in our children is to *be* outwardly and verbally positive in our own adult thinking and to fill our children's worlds with affirmations: "You've got this!" When it comes to supporting school success, positive talk is a simple but extremely powerful way to form positive thinking in their minds. That inner voice of "I've got this!" is crucial.

Another excellent way is to work hand in hand with your student's teachers. Just know that everything you do to promote positive talk at home is being backed up in the classroom with the consistent application of principles of assessment *for* learning. Your student is making a commitment to reaching clear and understandable learning goals, being consistently informed about their current achievement status, and getting to watch and reflect on gaps in their learning narrowing. Their sense of control, well-being, and confidence is improving. In that context, anything you can do to tune into these happenings and to stay in touch with your child's teacher will promote opportunities for positive affirmations.

This is especially important when you want to support your learner in working through some difficult learning. In this case, we need to be sure learning goals are set to be within reach for the student so they can get some wins and get on a winning streak and grow some confidence. A really helpful affirmation at home in this context is to talk with your child about how good it will be to have successfully worked though this challenge.

GUIDELINE 3: CELEBRATE SUCCESS

Yet another way to encourage positive thinking is to spotlight successes. This one is a very big emotional deal! Success defined either as hard-won small steps of progress or as hitting a really important learning target—such as mastering a really useful skill—serves as its own reward to be sure. But a big splashy acknowledgement helps too! Remember how I said that confidence doesn't just appear in our thinking as if by magic? Rather I said that it has to be earned? It is more likely to feel earned by the learner if we do two things: (1) celebrate each instance in some special way and (2) keep a cumulative record of successes so the pattern becomes visible and encouraging in its own right.

In addition, this kind of cumulative recordkeeping is even more valuable when it's built to reflect progress toward the attainment of a super-important learning goal. What if students build growth portfolios containing samples of work revealing how they have improved? What if this was in preparation for their student success conferences with parents? Early samples of their work revealed, "I wasn't good at this to begin with," while later samples said, "Look how much better I am doing." Such student-led parent conferences can be wonderful celebrations of achievement that give rise to hope for future success.

Our traditional focus of such celebrations has been good report cards. This definitely does deserve recognition. It's important. But we want something more. We want students to understand what those grades really mean about what they have learned and how they learned it. We need to celebrate everything that went into achieving the report card. Those lessons lay the groundwork for hope and future success.

GUIDELINE 4: FOCUS ON GROWTH

Throughout the first three guidelines, I have alluded to a thought that I want to make explicit. Let's center our attention as teachers and parents on change in student performance over time—on students doing better this time than they did before. Progress often happens in small but really important steps, not major leaps.

Students spend most of their time ascending the ladder to success and far less sitting on top of it.

We need to do everything in our power as parents and teachers to use ongoing self-assessment to help students see themselves successfully climbing the learning ladder so they can come to believe in themselves and so they will continue to be willing to do the work required to ascend to higher learning. They need to be able to take the risk of climbing, climb with confidence, and expect to succeed. And when they get there, let the bells ring out.

GUIDELINE 5: VOLUNTEER IN THE SCHOOL AND CLASSROOM

Whenever possible, you certainly can bring these four guidelines to bear in school settings. Sometimes teachers will welcome parents or members of the community as volunteers in their classrooms. These can represent opportunities to help teachers make sure that students know where they are headed in their learning, where they are now, and how they can close the gap between the two.

In a similar sense, participation in the parent–teacher association is always welcomed by school leaders and teachers. This too can afford opportunities to urge adoption of student-involved classroom assessment principles. Consider, for example, encouraging school leaders to adopt the idea represented in my earlier discussion of student-led parent–teacher success conferences. And finally, note that local school board meetings are public forums open to public input on how best to ensure maximum student learning success. Consider participating and offering your ideas.

CONCLUSION

I'm sure it has become clear to you that I am proposing a model of education and schooling that is different from the schools we experienced in our youth. I am not talking about merely ranking students at the end of high school based on their preparation to be confident lifelong learners. I am talking about universal lifelong learner confidence and competence. While their levels of achievement across school subjects will vary by the end of high school, and while we may still want to report those differences and consider them in helping them plan for their futures, their success in achieving their dreams in this rapidly changing world will turn on their willingness and ability to engage in lifelong learning.

Further, while the learning targets to be mastered include reading, writing, and arithmetic to be sure, our expectations now extend far beyond these and far beyond what was expected of us, and they will continue to expand. For this reason, anything we can do to make sure our students know what is expected of them from the very beginning of the learning and to help them believe they can hit those targets if they continue to strive will prepare them for the complex future they face.

Finally, as I have contended in previous chapters, we now understand why and how to use classroom testing as far more than a source of intimidation and anxiety to motivate effort and for the pursuit of report card grades. Now, to be sure, getting good grades is critically important. But researchers from around the world have helped us understand far more clearly today than did our teachers about how to maximize the chances of a student's success at learning. We set them up for maximum lifelong learning success by empowering them to manage their own success. We know how to do this.

Teacher–Parent Teamwork Suggestions

OK, teacher and parent teammates, at this point in the book you have read, hopefully understood, and discussed students' collaboration with their teachers as they monitor their own academic growth. I have argued as forcefully as I can that this partnership can have a profoundly positive impact on their achievement and the development of their self-confidence as learners. As a next step, I recommend that you see and hear these ideas in a different form. I have created a twenty-minute video summary of these basic ideas titled *Assessment for Student Learning and Confidence* (rickstiggins.com). Please discuss any new insights that come to you as a result of this presentation. Also, think about who else might benefit from seeing and hearing this video. Perhaps it can be used to introduce these ideas to local and state school leaders, as well as policy makers. They are the focus of my presentation in the next chapter.

CHAPTER 6

Actions for School Leaders and Policy Makers

"The way to develop self-confidence is to do the thing you fear and get a record of successful experiences behind you."

—William Jennings Bryan

As you will see, this chapter is entirely about "Teacher–Parent Teamwork Suggestions," all of which are intended to help you bring leaders at all levels on board with your school mission of helping every student become a confident, competent lifelong learner.

Teachers and parents, I am sure it has become increasingly obvious to you as you have been reading the previous chapters that success in bringing your teacher–student–parent teamwork into schools and classrooms will require support from those responsible for school leadership: school district instructional leaders, building principals, and local school district policy makers. This chapter describes specifically what we need from them and how to secure their commitment and help. I am counting on you as our student success team leaders to bring them on board.

Step one in that process is to help them understand that confidence in students is a foundation of their learning success. We want them to see that the instructional process of engaging students in ongoing self-monitoring and in managing their own learning is the key to helping them become confident lifelong learners. In other words, school leaders must come to see that ongoing classroom assessment can and must be far more than merely a source of grades—it can be an actual cause of learning.

The most efficient and effective way to introduce them to these ideas is to encourage them to team up with you to watch and discuss the twenty-minute video referenced at the end of Chapter 5 (see *Assessment for Student Learning and Confidence* at rickstiggins.com). Then invite them into working team study and discussion of this book.

From there, whether they are district- or building-level instructional leaders, they can support the development of strong teacher–student–parent partnerships by carrying out the actions listed and then detailed as follows.

1. Advance a two-part local school mission of maximizing student learning success while, at the same time, building confidence in students as learners

2. As supervisors of instruction, make student self-monitoring during learning a local instructional priority

3. To fulfill their responsibilities as supervisors of instruction, make sure all faculty members can gather dependable evidence of student achievement and are masters of the principles of assessment *for* learning

4. Build and maintain balanced local school district assessment systems—systems that meet the information needs of all instructional decision makers

5. As local school district leaders, make sure local, state, and federal educational policy makers understand the power of balanced assessment systems and of helping students take control of their own learning success

Here are some details to emphasize in encouraging these actions by your school leaders.

ACTION 1: SET A MISSION OF STUDENT SUCCESS AND CONFIDENCE

To review briefly from Chapter 1, historically, one mission of our schools has been to begin the process of sorting students into the various segments of our social and economic system by ranking them. Assessment's role has been to provide the evidence for ranking—assessment for triage, if you will.

Because of the rapid social and technological evolution of our culture, society wants (indeed needs) its schools to do more than rank. They also must help all students become well-equipped lifelong learners. Society demands that *all students*, not just a select few at the top of the rank order, master the fundamental reading, writing, math problem solving, and keys to success in the digital age. If all students are to be made ready for college or workplace training expectations, they all will need to be academically capable, and they must believe themselves capable of meeting those expectations whatever they may be.

If this two-part mission is to be fulfilled, all students must come to believe in themselves. Our communities must understand that, if struggling learners who have not yet met key standards give up in hopelessness, the new institutional mission of turning all students into lifelong learners cannot be fulfilled. It is crucial for everyone in the school community to understand these dynamics.

ACTION 2: PRIORITIZE INSTRUCTIONAL LEADERSHIP THAT BENEFITS TEACHERS

We have established that teachers spend a major proportion of their available professional time engaged in assessment-related activities. The quality of their work here has a direct impact on their learning success and confidence. These are critical dimensions of instruction—instruction for which the building principal is the responsible leader. This means that teachers need to be able to turn to their instructional leader for advice and guidance in the classroom assessment arena. It means that building principals are masters of the principles of sound practice in this domain. Further, if district instructional leaders are to supervise the work of building principals, they too must be masters of those principles.

To be specific, principals must be prepared to observe and evaluate a teacher's assessment *for* learning practices and to provide feedback on strengths and areas in need of improvement. Principals need to provide or arrange professional development experiences for those teachers who wish to advance their own classroom assessment literacy. In another sense, principals must be prepared to address the community in a clear and convincing manner about sound practices. This requires classroom-assessment-literate principals who are ready to provide instructional leadership to benefit their teachers.

I strongly recommend that school and district leaders authentically partner with teachers to evaluate local assessment systems and provide the professional learning needed to make those systems operational in their schools. This has profound implications for the development of academically capable and confident students.

ACTION 3: PREPARE TO MONITOR CONTINUOUS STUDENT GROWTH

We have established that confidence grows in learners when they know where they're headed and when they get to watch themselves coming ever closer to getting there. This means they see the learning pathway laid out before them, and they see themselves moving past the signposts as they learn. If there is no pathway—no signposts or no evidence for them to interpret as their progress—then there is no basis for making the self-judgment that "I've got this. I am OK. I'm going to keep trying." There is no basis for building confidence.

The basis for this journey metaphor is the curriculum. Both within and across classrooms, learning targets must be arrayed in progressions to unfold over time as learning unfolds. Teachers must be confident, competent masters of the learning targets their students are expected to master. And those targets must be transformed into student- and family-friendly versions to be shared with students and their families from the very beginning of the learning. These are the foundations of preparation to monitor and promote continuous student growth.

Another foundation was announced in Action 2. The faculty will need to be able to monitor (assess) students' progress as they learn in order to track growth *with* and *for* students and their families. Let me add just a bit more detail about what this means. Those who are prepared to gather good evidence can do the following:

1. Choose an *appropriate assessment method* given the learning target(s) to be assessed (options include paper and pencil testing, essay assessment, and performance assessments. The method of choice depends on the learning target)

2. Gather a *sample of performance* large enough to support a confident inference about each student's mastery of the target(s) in question

3. Build using only *high-quality assessment exercises and scoring schemes*

4. Avoid *potential sources of bias* that can distort assessment results and misrepresent achievement

These standards of assessment quality apply regardless of context. It is not possible dependably to track student growth either by student or by teacher if these quality control standards are not met in the classroom.

And finally with respect to centering on student growth, the results of the monitoring process must be communicated to students in a timely and understandable form that makes progress apparent to them. This is where the basic principles of assessment *for* learning described in Chapter 3 come into play. If students see and understand the target from the beginning of instruction, develop a sense of the pathway they will be traveling to success, develop at least the beginnings of a vocabulary that permits them to communicate about those targets, and understand how the evidence they will be receiving along the way connects to their pathway, then it becomes possible to reveal their own growth to them as it is happening. Feedback will have meaning and will clarify for them what comes next in their learning. The result is increasingly confident learners.

I fully realize that the traditional means of comunicating about student achievement has been the report card grading system. But as you will see in Action 4 to follow, this way of communicating falls in the summative assessment column of a balanced local assessment system. It is important. Grades must accurately reflect levels of student achievement at the time of reporting. But we also need to help students grow so they can achieve those good grades at reporting time. This too is part of a truly balanced local assessment system.

ACTION 4: BALANCE YOUR LOCAL DISTRICT ASSESSMENT SYSTEM

Clearly, the applications of assessment described in the previous chapters place day-to-day classroom assessment *for* student learning at center stage and in the spotlight. In this case, the prime users are teachers and their students, with parents also playing a key role. Obviously, this extends the use of assessment far beyond its role in providing evidence for grading or for test score accountability. It's not that these applications are unimportant. But it does mean that, if assessment (the process of gathering information to inform educational decisions) is to serve us well, it must serve the *full array* of important users and uses.

Let's review who the users are. There are decision makers at the classroom level serving students and teachers; at the level of interim benchmark assessments serving teacher *teams*, building administrators, and district instructional leaders; and with annual standardized tests serving school and district leaders and policy makers. No single assessment can meet the needs of this diverse array of decision makers. More about that will follow.

Now, let's analyze the diverse array of instructional decisions that make up the schooling process. Sometimes we use the assessment process and its results to support student learning as described in earlier chapters. When these users are teachers, let's call this *formative assessment*. They rely on evidence to plan instruction to meet student needs. But when teachers team up with their students during learning to plan instruction, we'll label this *assessment for learning*. And, finally, some users rely on assessment evidence to judge the sufficiency of learning given preset expectations. These are *summative assessment* contexts involving teachers, building leaders, district leaders, and policy makers.

Now we have in hand the ingredients needed to outline a truly balanced local school district assessment system designed and developed to serve all users and uses. Table 6.1 crosses the three groups of users identified earlier with our three kinds of uses to produce a nine-cell representation of an assessment system built to serve all users well. Within each cell are listed the important user(s) in that context, an instructional decision to be made, and the kind of information assessment needs to provide to help them decide.

TABLE 6.1 ● Framework of a Balanced Local District Assessment System

LEVEL/PURPOSE	FORMATIVE ASSESSMENT FOR MANAGEMENT OF INSTRUCTION	ASSESSMENT FOR LEARNING	SUMMATIVE ASSESSMENT OF LEARNING
Classroom Assessment 1. *Key decision maker(s)* 2. *Important instructional decisions to be made* 3. *Information needed to inform decisions*	1. Teacher 2. What comes next in my students' learning? 3. Evidence of standards mastered and not yet mastered	1. Student–teacher team 2. Help student know: What comes next in my learning? 3. Evidence of student's current place in progressions	1. Teacher 2. What grade should be put on student's report card? 3. Evidence of student mastery of each required standard
Periodic Benchmark Tests 1. *Key decision maker(s)* 2. *Important instructional decisions to be made* 3. *Information needed to inform decisions*	1. Teachers and instructional leaders in professional learning communities 2. Which standards do we tend to struggle with mastering, and why? 3. Evidence of standards not mastered across classrooms	1. Curriculum and instructional leaders and teacher teams, but students might also assist in interpreting results 2. Which standards are our students struggling to master, and why? 3. Evidence of standards not mastered across classrooms	1. Curriculum and instructional leaders 2. Which standards are not being mastered? 3. Evidence of standards not mastered across classrooms

LEVEL/PURPOSE	FORMATIVE ASSESSMENT FOR MANAGEMENT OF INSTRUCTION	ASSESSMENT FOR LEARNING	SUMMATIVE ASSESSMENT OF LEARNING
Annual Tests 1. *Key decision maker(s)* 2. *Important instructional decisions to be made* 3. *Information needed to inform decisions*	1. Curriculum and instructional leaders 2. What standards are our students not mastering, and why? 3. Evidence of standards not mastered	*There is no viable assessment for learning role for annual tests*	1. District leadership team, school board, and community 2. Did enough of our students master required standards? 3. Percentage of students mastering standards

Source: Adapted from Stiggins, R. (2017). The perfect assessment system. ASCD.

Please take a few minutes to review this table. As you see this big picture, where do you believe the decisions are made that exert the greatest impact on student learning success and academic well-being? Yet, in which cells have we invested the preponderance of our assessment resources over the past several decades? Do you see the problem here?

The only cells in this table that include uses of assessment that have been linked in rigorous scientific research to significant gains in student achievement are in the formative and assessment *for* learning used day-to-day in the classroom. But the cells that have attracted the greatest investment of our state and federal assessment resources are the summative cells at the bottom, expenditures for developing, administering, scoring, and reporting standardized test scores. It's difficult to find rigorous scientific evidence of a link between this application of assessment and gains in student achievement.

Now let me hasten to add that this is not an argument for doing away with such summative tests. They serve valuable purposes of identifying important learning deficits and allocating resources at the program level. But we must understand that our assessment system habits have been grossly out of balance in the allocation of resources given their expected impact on student well-being.

This calls for strong leadership at the local school district level. I recommend that a district team to include teachers, parents, school/district instructional leaders, and school board members audit the balance of local systems and rebalance if needed. When this carefully balanced local system has been designed, present the plan to the school board for community review and approval. State and federal resources for the refinement of assessment systems can be used for this. Let the community know that this work is being done and why.

If the mission of schools is to make every student ready for college or workplace training, and if we know that classroom assessment is the application that can contribute the most to delivering on that mission, then the mission of this district oversight team is clear: make sure every user of assessment to inform instructional decisions at every level (especially the classroom) has access to dependable evidence while the learning is happening so they can use it to build confident lifelong learners.

ACTION 5: EDUCATE POLICY MAKERS

Some policy makers are professional educators, such as staff members in state departments of education. However, their professional learning experiences often lack basic assessment literacy training. Further, many educational policy makers, such as school board members or legislators, are not trained in this domain of professional practice either, especially as those practices are described in this book. These school and community leaders need to be schooled in sound instructional practices in order to set policies that guide sound practices. It falls to local teacher and school leaders to train them. There is no other option. And, it falls to parents and other members of the local school community to demand those sound policies and practices.

What follows is a story from an educational policy–leadership context that illustrates how one high school faculty helped their school board understand the meaning of effective instructional practice:

Visualize yourself at a particularly important meeting of the school board of your local school district. This is the once-a-year meeting at which the local school leaders present the annual report of standardized test scores to the board and the media. Every year it's the same: Will scores be up or down? How will you compare to national norms? How will your schools compare to others in the area?

What attendees this evening can't realize as the meeting begins is that, this year, they are in for a big surprise with respect to both the achievement information to be presented and the manner of the presentation.

The audience includes a young woman named Sofia, a junior at the high school, sitting in the back of the room with her parents. She knows she will be a big part of the surprise. She's only a little nervous. She understands how important her role is.

The district leaders begin by reminding the attendees that the standardized tests sample broad domains of achievement with just a few multiple-choice test items. But many important outcomes of teaching cannot be measured in that way. So sometimes other methods must be used. They promise to provide an example later in the presentation.

Having set the stage, the school leaders turn to carefully prepared charts depicting average student performance in each important achievement category tested. Results are summarized by grade and building, concluding with a clear description of how district results have changed from the year before and from previous years. As the presenters proceed, board members ask questions and receive clarification. Some scores are down slightly; some are up. Participants discuss possible reasons. This is a routine annual presentation that proceeds as expected.

Next comes the break from routine. The presenters explain how the schools have gathered some new information about one important aspect of student achievement. The school leaders and faculty have implemented a new writing program to address the issue of inadequate writing skills among graduates. The English faculty completed a training program on assessing writing proficiency and integrating such assessments into the teaching and learning process.

For the second half of the evening's assessment presentation, the high school English department faculty shares the results of their evaluation of the new writing program. The English chair, Ms. Williams, distributes a sample of student writing to the board members (student's name removed), asking them to read and evaluate this writing. They do so, expressing their dismay aloud. They're indignant in their commentary on these samples of student work. One board member reports in exasperation that the new writing program is not working. This is a pretty weak performance. Sofia's mom puts her arm around her daughter's shoulder and hugs her.

Ms. Williams distributes another sample of student writing, asking the board to read and evaluate it. Ah, this, they report, is more like it! This work is much better! But be specific, the chair demands. What do you like about this work? They list positive aspects: good choice of words, sound sentence structure, clever ideas, and so on. Sofia is ready to burst!

The reason she's so full of pride at this moment is that this has been a special year for her and her classmates. For the first time ever, they became partners with their English teacher, Ms. Weathersby, in managing their own improvement as writers. Early in the year, Ms. W (to the students) made it crystal clear to Sofia that she was, in fact, not a very good writer and that just trying hard to get better was not going to be enough. She expected Sofia to be better—nothing else would suffice.

Ms. W started the year by helping students set high writing standards for word choice, sentence structure, organization, voice, and so on. She defined each of these in student-friendly terms with examples of good- and poor-quality writing. When Sofia and her teacher evaluated her first two pieces of writing using these standards, she received very low ratings. Not very good.

But she also began to study samples of good writing, and slowly she began to understand why they were good. The differences between these and her work started to become clear to her. Ms. W shared strategies that would help her writing improve one step at a time. Sofia and her classmates learned to provide feedback to each other focused on the characteristics of good writing they had learned. As time passed, they kept samples of their work in their growth portfolios so they could compare their old writing to their new writing. Sofia's writing skills were improving before her very eyes. It was a very good year.

Now, having set the board up by having them analyze, evaluate, and compare these two samples of student work provided, Ms. W springs the surprise: The two pieces of writing they have just evaluated, one of lesser quality and one of outstanding quality, were produced by the same writer at the beginning and at the end of the school year. This, she reports, is evidence of the kind of impact the new writing program is having on student writing proficiency.

Needless to say, all are impressed. However, one board member wonders aloud, "Have all your students improved in this way?" Having anticipated the question, the rest of the English faculty joins the presentation and produces carefully prepared charts depicting dramatic changes in typical student performance over time on rating scales for each of six clearly articulated dimensions of good writing.

Further, Ms. W informs the board that the student whose improvement has been so dramatically illustrated in the work they have just seen is present at this school board meeting, along with her parents. This student is ready to talk with the board about the nature of her learning experience. Sofia, you're on!

Interest among the board members runs high. Sofia talks about how she has come to understand the truly important differences between good and bad writing. She refers to differences she had not understood before, how she has learned to assess her own writing and to fix it when it doesn't "work well," and how she and her classmates have learned to talk with her teacher and each other about what it means to write well. She contends that Ms. W believed in them and that helped them become confident writers.

School board attention turns to their teacher. Ms. W talks about the improved focus of writing instruction, increase in student motivation, and important positive changes in the very nature of the student–teacher relationship.

A board member asks Sofia if she likes to write. She reports, "I do now!" This board member turns to Sofia's parents and asks for their impression of all this. They report with pride that they had never before seen so much evidence of Sofia's achievement, and most of it came from Sofia herself. Sofia had never been called on to lead the parent–teacher conference before. They had no idea she was so articulate—her growth portfolio of work really showed marked improvement. They loved it. Their daughter's pride in and accountability for achievement had skyrocketed in the past year.

By helping her students engage in ongoing self-monitoring in just these ways, Ms. Weathersby accomplished two things. First, she turned the keys to the kingdom regarding good writing—an essential lifelong learner skill—over to her students, lock, stock, and barrel. Second, in doing so, she brought the kind of positive emotional dynamics we discussed in Chapters 2 and 3 to life in her classroom in support of the learning success of her students. Sofia and her classmates gained a strong sense of control over their own academic well-being.

As we already have established, federal and state policy makers have directed that *all* students are to be made "ready for college or workplace training." Given the evolution of our culture, we know that they will need this to survive, let alone prosper. This was not the mission of the schools in which most adults of today grew up. Times have changed, and our political leaders are to be applauded for redefining the social mission of our schools to serve these changing times. But it has been clear over the decades that merely holding students accountable for annual test scores has not done and cannot do the job by itself. It is time for local, state, and federal educational policy makers to stop believing and acting like it can.

Those who set educational policy must understand the implications of the previously stated mission of leaving no child behind. It means that the emotional dynamics underpinning school success for students must leave every student believing in themselves. They must be given the opportunity to learn to control their own learning success. This means that they must experience sufficient success in school that they come truly to believe success is due to their own efforts. This attribution is foundational to becoming a confident lifelong learner. Therefore, as I have said in earlier chapters and repeat again now, we can no longer have any students giving up in hopelessness.

The way to instill in students this sense of confidence and control over their success is by actually teaching them how to exercise that control in the classroom while they are learning. We can do this, in effect, by holding up a mirror so they can watch themselves succeeding due to their efforts. That mirror is student-involved classroom assessment *for* learning. Its power to motivate and advance learning success is unquestioned worldwide. As you have learned in earlier chapters, it's based on making sure students always know the answer to three questions as they grow: Where am I headed in my learning? Where am I now? How can I close the gap? The path to success is clear. This permits them to see progress unfolding for them. Success always is within reach if they try. In this way, we give them the gift of confidence.

Those school leaders who are interested in their own development in sound assessment practices will find valuable assistance in the following resources:

- Chappuis, S., Brookhart, S., & Chappuis, J. (2021). *Ten assessment literacy goals for school leaders.* Corwin.

  The authors provide school leaders with a process for conducting their own step-by-step self-analysis of the current level of their assessment literacy along with guidelines for personal professional development in this domain.

- Stiggins, R. (2017). *The perfect assessment system.* ASCD.

  Those interested in evaluating the balance of their own local school district's assessment system and in adjusting that balance as needed will find practical assistance here.

THANK YOU

Teachers, parents, school leaders, and policy makers, I began our exploration of the link between achievement and academic confidence with the stories of my early failure and loss of faith in myself as a learner. But my teachers rekindled my hope, which encouraged me to take the risk of trying! Success followed through a lifetime for which I will be eternally thankful. But the thing is, we know how to make this dream come true for every young learner! We need only to embrace this mission and commit to its fulfillment. This will take a community-wide effort.

Teachers, I know you can and will take the lead. Thank you for that. You know that you create the future with your work. You have been advocating a better assessment future for decades now. Your time is at hand. Bring our students and their parents with you now as we create that better vision of learned, confident students.

Parents, I know that no one has more hope for the well-being of your children than you. I'm with you. Our mission as parents is to keep them on a positive pathway to success, confidence, and happiness. I'm sure it is no surprise to you that success is first in that list. You are a major player in your child's journey to academic success. Thank you for that.

Local school leaders, I know you seek to comply with the demands for higher test scores as you should. We can get there, but only if your learners come to believe in themselves. Please forgive my frankness as I demand and I am asking that your communities demand that you balance your local assessment systems. The classroom is key, because it is only there that we can attend to the information needs of your teachers and their students.

School board members and legislators, I know you stand for the truly effective schools. Thank you for that. But merely measuring effectiveness obviously hasn't done it. We must seek day-to-day learning success, which leads to confidence, which leads to more success, which leads to . . . you see where this goes. I am certain this is what you want too. The key is student–teacher success–confidence partnerships.

Villagers, your mission is clear. Carry on.

NEA Task Force Principles for the Future of Assessment

1. *Create community-based and student-centered processes for assessing student growth, learning, and development.*

   a. Engage the community—including students, families, caregivers, educators, policymakers, and other stakeholders—in a process to grow knowledge about assessing what students know and can do.

   b. Collaborate with stakeholders to establish shared beliefs and values about the various purposes, methods, and outcomes of assessment.

   c. Rely on educator expertise to guide the community in establishing consensus on appropriate assessment for various purposes.

   d. Together, with the community and students, contribute to determinations about what is assessed by identifying shared values and determining how we define and measure "success."

   e. Share high-quality, contextualized information about individual and schoolwide student achievements in a way that informs stakeholders and provides the data needed in order to make informed decisions to support student learning and success.

2. *Prioritize assuring all educators are trained in assessment literacy and are able to ensure racially and culturally relevant and responsive assessment that meets the needs of all students and centers their full identities.*

   a. Implement high-quality systems that make equity and the expertise, knowledge, and experiences of educators inherent in the creation of classroom, local, and statewide assessment.

   b. Utilize local knowledge and resources to integrate assessment systems that encompass both globally recognized competencies (knowledge, skills, and values that allow students to thrive in a diverse and interdependent world) and learning goals as well as local practices, values, and contexts.

   c. Design assessment at all levels—including classroom, district, and statewide assessment—with educators who are steeped in assessment literacy and antiracist assessment practices.

   d. Ensure that educators have the time, support, resources, and knowledge to create, implement, evaluate, and communicate a full array of assessment methods and assessment results, including deepening the use of low-stakes, curriculum-embedded, and formative assessment practices.

3. *Design assessment that inspires learning. Assess what is meaningful to student well-being, learning, and individuality.*

   a. Place students at the center of our transformation of assessment systems to focus on assessing as a form of learning, increase student self-evaluation, and support student self-efficacy.

   b. Increase the use of appropriate assessment methods, given the intended learning goals and purposes, which fit the context to gather holistic information about individual and institutional opportunities for student learning, growth, and success.

    c. Ensure that all students have opportunities to develop and demonstrate higher-order thinking and problem-solving skills, including, but not limited to, self-evaluation and peer-evaluation methods.

    d. Communicate and discuss assessment results with individual students in a language and format that is clear, understandable, and actionable in order to foster student self-efficacy and ownership of learning.

4. *Utilize multiple sources and kinds of evidence of student learning to contribute to decisions on student promotion, retention, course grades and enrollment, and graduation.*

    a. Value the assets that students bring to school.

    b. Ensure an antiracist approach in the design and administration of assessment to ensure fairness in the creation, administration, and evaluation of assessment for student learning.

    c. Decouple federally mandated statewide student assessment from high-stakes consequences for students, schools, and educators to help ensure that no one measure should be used to determine a student's performance or access to supports and opportunities.

    d. Make student promotion and retention decisions based on a combination of evidence from a variety of sources. Potential sources include educator recommendations; a representative sample of student work, which may include assessment; and conversations with students, families and caregivers, specialized instructional support personnel, and other stakeholders.

5. *Provide students, educators, and schools with the resources needed to put these principles into action, with opportunities for all students to demonstrate their knowledge, creativity, and skills.*

a. Equip facilities and personnel with ample and equitable resources, materials, funding, tools, etc. to ensure that results are comparable and accurately reflect the knowledge and skills of all students across school sites.
b. Provide equitable opportunities to expand student assessment systems to include a diverse variety of assessment methods. All methods of assessment should be free of cultural, racial, gender, and other biases, and they should be evaluated regularly to prevent negative impacts based on identities.
c. Support the administration of a well-rounded system of assessment by assuring accommodations, adaptations (including appropriate time and technology, for example), exemptions, and ample flexibilities to give all students the opportunity to demonstrate their knowledge and skills.
d. Assess with full and appropriate accommodations, modifications, exemptions, and flexibilities for multilingual students and students with disabilities.
e. Ensure that methods of assessing do not disrupt learning for extended periods, especially for multilingual learners and students with disabilities.

References

Austin, T. (1994). *Changing the view: Student-led parent conferences.* Heinemann.

Bandura, A. (1994). Self-efficacy. In V. S. Ramachaudran (Ed.), *Encyclopedia of human behavior* (Vol. 4, pp. 71–81). Academic Press.

Black, P. (2013). Formative and summative aspects of assessment: Theoretical and research foundations in the context of pedagogy. In J. McMillan (Ed.), *Sage handbook of research on classroom assessment* (pp. 167–178). Sage.

Black, P., & Wiliam, D. (1998a). Assessment and classroom learning. *Assessment in Education, 5*(1), 7–71.

Black, P., & Wiliam, D. (1998b). Inside the black box: Raising standards through classroom assessment. *Phi Delta Kappan, 80*(2), 139–148.

Chappuis, J. (2015). *Seven strategies of assessment for learning* (2nd ed.). Pearson.

Chappuis, J., & Stiggins, R. (2017). *An introduction to student-involved assessment for learning* (7th ed.). Pearson.

Chappuis, J., & Stiggins, R. (2020). *Classroom assessment for student learning: Doing it right, using it well* (3rd ed.). Pearson.

Chappuis, S., Brookhart, S., & Chappuis, J. (2021). *Ten assessment literacy goals for school leaders.* Corwin.

Dweck, C. (2007, November 28). The secret to raising smart kids. *Scientific American Mind.*

Kanter, R. M. (2004). *Confidence: How winning streaks and losing streaks begin and end.* Crown Business.

NEA Task Force on the Future of Assessment. (2022, February 4). https://www.nea.org/sites/default/files/2022-06/Principles%20for%20the%20Future%20of%20Assessment.pdf

Sadler, D. R. (1998). Formative assessment: Revisiting the territory. *Assessment in Education, 5*(1), 77–84.

Stiggins, R. (2014). *Revolutionize assessment: Engage students, inspire learning.* Corwin.

Stiggins, R. (2017). *The perfect assessment system.* ASCD.

Stiggins, R., & Conklin, N. (1992). *In teachers' hands: Investigating the practice of classroom assessment.* SUNY Press.

Wiliam, D., Lee, C., Harrison, C., & Black, P. (2004). Teachers developing assessment for learning: Impact on student achievement. *Assessment in Education: Principles, Policy, and Practice, 11*(1), 49–65.

Index

A Sage Company

CORWIN HAS ONE MISSION: to enhance education through intentional professional learning.

We build long-term relationships with our authors, educators, clients, and associations who partner with us to develop and continuously improve the best evidence-based practices that establish and support lifelong learning.